A Word about the Cover Art...

We stumbled upon Jan Vermeer's *Christ in the House of Mary and Martha* at a busy book convention with our publisher, Roy Carlisle, after searching all day for cover images in mild frustration. The three of us liked it immediately, moved by its contrast with how we were feeling on that day amid the overwhelming visual stimuli, noise, and the brush of people everywhere.

It dawned on us that Mary and Martha, like us, were indeed two very different women with unique approaches to prayer. Soon, the rich imagery of these two gospel women began to work its way into our hearts and psyches as symbols of what happens when women pray. To us they look satisfied yet hungry, attentive yet distracted, receptive yet giving, exhibiting that rich mix of emotion and intellect that makes women so special and so diverse. In this particular painting, Mary, seated humbly at the feet of Jesus, symbolizes prayerfulness. Martha, always known as the busy one, is serving, but she is also listening. Her role of service is vital as well. In fact, she's bringing bread, symbolic of the Eucharist, to the table. In this chosen setting, she is moving toward what is essential in life, a "Mary" attitude of loving contemplation and surrender, drawing closely to the One who can accomplish that work in her soul.

As we prayed with the images, Mary and Martha became all the gospel women who were treated with dignity and respect as they walked with Jesus. They became the women who traveled daily with him, broke bread with him, learned from him — and yes, taught him about themselves and their lives. They became those of us today who also welcome Jesus with all our hearts as we long for healing, connection, and meaningfulness, seeking to find "the better part" as our busy lives continually flourish and change.

For in truth, there is Mary and Martha within each of us. We seek the place where Mary and Martha — contemplation and a heart for service — meet within us, a God-point of grace and transformation. For as we embrace all the parts of ourselves in love and step out in faith, we become fully — *women who pray.*

When Women Pray

As Jesus and his disciples
went on their way,
he came to a village
where a woman named Martha
welcomed him in her home.
She had a sister named Mary,
who sat down at the feet of the Lord
and listened to his teaching. (GNT)

When Women Pray

Our Personal Stories
of Extraordinary Grace

LYN HOLLEY DOUCET
AND ROBIN HEBERT

A Crossroad Book
The Crossroad Publishing Company
New York

The Crossroad Publishing Company
16 Penn Plaza, 481 Eighth Avenue
New York, NY 10001

Scripture quotations labeled NRSV are from the New Revised Standard Version Bible, copyright © 1993 by the Division of Christian Education of the National Council of the Churches of Christ in the U.S.A. Used by permission. All rights reserved.

Scripture quotations labeled NAB are from the New American Bible, copyright © 1991, 1986, 1970 by the Confraternity of Christian Doctrine, 3211 Fourth Street, N.E., Washington, D.C. 20017-1194. All rights reserved.

Scripture quotations labeled GNT are from the Good News Translation in Today's English Version, Second Edition, © 1992 by American Bible Society. Used by permission. All rights reserved.

The text fonts are Sabon, Goudy Sans, and Benguiat.
The display font is Liberty.

Printed in the United States of America

Library of Congress Cataloging-in-Publication Data
Doucet, Lyn Holley, 1950-
    When women pray : our personal stories of extraordinary grace /
Lyn Holley Doucet and Robin Hebert.
        p.   cm.
    Includes bibliographical references (p.   ).
    ISBN 0-8245-2279-6 (alk. paper)
    1. Catholic women – Religious life. 2. Spiritual life – Catholic Church.
3. Prayer – Catholic Church. 4. Doucet, Lyn Holley, 1950- 5. Hebert,
Robin. I. Hebert, Robin. II. Title.
BX2353.D68 2004
248.3′2′082 – dc22
                                                      2004021257

1 2 3 4 5 6 7 8 9 10   10 09 08 07 06 05 04

From Robin...
To my daughters, Megan and Emily, and to all those *daughters*
to whom I long to pass on my love of God.

And to my sister Theresians,
who have taught me the most about prayer.

From Lyn...
For those who walk with me in faith:
my directees, spiritual brothers and sisters,
and all whose souls touch mine.

Contents

We Invite You to a Life of Prayer

All we have to give away is our own journey, our own story. Then we become living witnesses. The only authority we have in other people's lives is what we ourselves have walked and what we know to be true. Then we have earned the right to speak.

—Richard Rohr, *Everything Belongs*

LHD It is early morning, as I sip my coffee and ponder the introduction to our emerging book. All around me are books: on shelves, in baskets, in teetering stacks on the floor. Most of them speak of the spiritual journey, which has been for me a path to more wholeness and freedom in my life.

This morning I am intensely aware of the community of readers and writers to which I belong, separated by time and distance, yet one in our hearts. My journey has been shaped by the generous sharing of writers: Fr. William Barry, C. S. Lewis, Sr. Joyce Rupp, Paula D'Arcy, Melody Beatty, Sue Monk Kidd, Fr. Richard Rohr, and Sr. Macrina Wiederkehr. The list goes on. Reading their pages has helped me to feel less alone, less strange. I have felt embraced by their questing hearts, so much like my own. These were my mentors, the voyagers who longed to be closer to God, to peer into mystery, and to examine their life experiences in the illuminative grace of faith.

I remember clearly the day I read some simple words from Fr. William Barry. I don't remember the exact phrases, but the meaning was, "Life is a spiritual journey. There is a path that has been prepared for you." My heart lifted with hope. Could it be that there is a path for me? That God loves me enough to be guiding my steps? The more I offered myself to this path, the more I was sure it existed and the more that I knew that a passionate God was intimately involved in my daily life.

In love, these writers gave their best; and in love Robin and I long to do the same for others. Though millions of words have been written about the journey of prayer and faith, I believe that Robin and I bring something authentic to this quest: our own unique and lived experiences as married women, living in families with children, connected to our local communities and professions. Robin's road and mine have been much the same and much different.

We both have an educator's background and share the vocation of spiritual direction. Robin offers her ministry on a busy college campus; I lead directees in the quiet setting of my country home. I work in music ministry in my own parish, and Robin does just about everything in hers! Our adult lives have been lived out in marriage and family. My marriage began in 1971, the fruit of a blind date, but Robin is the survivor of a painful divorce, although she is now in a four-year loving and life-giving marriage. My trial came with my infertility, and I am the grateful mother of one much-loved son, conceived after medical intervention. However, my longing for additional children was not fulfilled. Robin raised four children, ages seven to thirteen at the time of her separation, and experienced the heartrending challenges and trials of single motherhood.

Today, the blessings of close-knit children, a loving husband, stepchildren, and grandchildren are a source of growth and many miracles in her life.

Both the painful times and the fruitful times have put us on the road to writing this book. We see in each other differences that we cherish and oneness of purpose that unites us. Thomas Merton tells us, "Home roots us in eternity. It is the symbol of our final integration; we achieve perfect wholeness in God. This is the deepest meaning of going home." As we daily come home to God's mercy and love, we long to gently guide others along paths home.

We are two women of ordinary circumstances who have had, through God's grace, extraordinary experiences in prayer. We have been tossed through stormy days and sailed into harbors of peace and joy. We have tasted despair and experienced amazing transcendence. We have encountered all the everydays, when nothing much seems to be happening within, when weariness and boredom reign. And yet we have a sweet fire that burns within us, even when banked low. We have been changed by Love. We offer our experiences, not as a template for others, but as a gentle path of encouragement.

—L.H.D.

RH Gifted by the light and wisdom of those who have gone before us and graced by the direction of wise guides along the way, Lyn and I have encountered a God who not only loves us unconditionally but also a God who is graciously involved in our daily lives. As spiritual directors, we are privileged to walk with others as they discover deeply who God is for them.

There is never a story shared by another that doesn't transform my own life in some sort of way, that doesn't reach down into the belly of my own soul and provide some healing, word of encouragement, or slice of joy. As author Joyce Rupp says, "We can discover our home when we discover another's story of seeking." That's what stories do. They bring us home.

My tattered copy of Macrina Wiederkehr's *A Tree Full of Angels* speaks of my own homecoming many years ago. The book was a gift, perhaps one of the greatest I ever received. I was struggling with an emptiness triggered by the release of years of grief surrounding a painful betrayal. Macrina's words filled my longing soul with an inconceivable hope: "My yearning for God has been so deep lately. It's been an ache that I cannot reach. Today the God I couldn't reach reached me — reached into my inner soul and showed me my speck of eternal life."

God reached *me*. God reached me in spite of my struggle with unworthiness and my battle with feeling unwelcomed. On a sunny spring morning, Macrina's touching words, lifted right out of her own journey, provided a Knowing that I was home with God. Finally.

Writer Henri Nouwen says that the heart of the spiritual battle is to know that we are welcomed. We are welcomed to know the heart of our Creator and to be at home there. Darker spirits within will try to convince us that we don't have a place there, that we are not worthy of this much love, that we can't be fully received by God.

In our essays we hope to convey another message: *Don't be afraid. This life of faith that we have experienced is offered to everyone! Come and be filled! Come and be made whole!* Come and be at home!

We freely share with you our own experiences with God as they have unfolded day by day. We stand as witnesses to our own stories of healing and conversion, offering you an invitation to journey with us to an unseen world of wonderful and amazing experiences in prayer. Just as God continues to yearn for us, he yearns for you.

With open hearts, we offer you a life of prayer.   —R.H.

Lord, Teach Me to Pray

We need not worry about "spiritual growth." We need only build rhythms into our lives that enable us to live in tune with the Spirit; the Spirit then does the rest, drawing us closer to the Lord both in prayer and in service. —Richard J. Hauser, S.J., *In His Spirit*

In the morning, while it was still very dark, he got up and went out to a deserted place, and there he prayed. —Mark 1:35 NRSV

RH I will never forget my initial meeting with my first "official" spiritual director, Fr. Hampton Davis. Excited and a bit nervous about the appointment, I strutted into his office with props in my hands: time-management book, journal, favorite spiritual book, and purse, all stacked like the tower of Babylon. I greeted Fr. Hampton with the unspoken message "Now teach me!" as if prayer were a subject about which I could just ingest information and then repeat on a test. He politely removed my armor, placing the burdensome stack on the floor, and then sat me down to pray. I felt stripped and naked, as he reached for my hands and spoke an opening prayer. His comforting words awakened my hurried spirit to that priceless moment, offering a sense of safety I hadn't felt in years. My tight-fisted heart relaxed in his loving care as Father tenderly dried my tears, asking what about the prayer had touched me. The word "reverence" had wrapped around my soul.

14

"What does 'reverence' mean to you, Robin?"

"Respect . . . respect for God, I guess."

"Robin, but you don't have a clue about how to respect yourself!" he lovingly suggested. "You're too busy being the good little mother, counselor, and volunteer that you have forgotten how to take care of yourself — *really* take care of yourself."

He explained to me that self-reverence is a clear commandment of God and that it arises from the inside out. There is nothing I can do to *earn* reverence. Fr. Hampton helped me to see that the greatest way I could feel reverence for myself was to become a receiver of God's love. He spoke of the saints as those who had learned to let God love them and suggested that we are all called to be saints. He proposed that I wouldn't find sainthood in my *doing* for God but in deepening my prayer life. I left his office with a promise to begin.

I decided that each morning would be designated time for God, a sort of Sabbath for an hour or so. I would snuggle in my cream-colored linen chair with the aqua piping that sat in my bedroom. It was not only soft and comfortable, but also contained in its fabric the essence of its previous owner, my mother. She had sat in it to embroider beautiful smocked garments that she skillfully created. I sat in it to embroider my soul. My prayer chair, as I came to call it, offered a perfect view of the tall maple tree outside my second-story window. That late autumn, the tree seemed to be shedding for me the layers of pain I felt, my sense of deep unworthiness, my resistance to silence and solitude. Some mornings, as I practiced centering prayer, tears flowed like a cleansing rain. Other mornings, I struggled simply to stay awake. As the weeks passed, however,

I became aware of a deep longing in me for God. What a delight to discover God's yearning for me!

Every session with Fr. Hampton involved engaging in the question of how my daily prayer was coming along. Sometimes I had to admit that I had prayed only twice during the week, but he would faithfully remind me: "Robin, it's difficult to hear God's voice driving down Johnston Street!" a main thoroughfare in Lafayette. He delightfully suggested that if my time for God is 8:00 a.m., then God is there at 7:00, excitedly declaring, "Yes! She's coming!" How could I want anything less than to meet him there?

Months later, as Lent approached, I was still struggling with the daily discipline of prayer, so it occurred to me that instead of *giving up* a substance as a Lenten observance, I could fast from the belief that I didn't have enough time each day for prayer. It worked. I was simply amazed by the many fruits of prayer: the incredible "God instances," the meaningful coincidences where I could not deny God's faithful reassurance that I am never really alone, the healing words I was rediscovering in Scripture, the surprise encounter with God's very presence deep within my being. Those six weeks became ten years — indeed, some of the most fulfilling of my life. That Lent was the beginning, the advent of a whole new era in my life in which an entirely fresh and life-giving relationship with myself and with God was born.

The journey, of course, continues, as a path of yearning and gratification, intimacy and withdrawal, filled with some of the most tender moments of my life as well as some of the most excruciatingly painful. Very often there is nothing that occurs in my time set apart for prayer. I'm just aware of a deep sense of peace that pervades my spirit throughout the day. There are also days when I draw on the graces of strength to suffer through a tough situation or prudence to say or do the right thing. I am often graced with patience to bear a certain trial, or sheer joy from the thankful recognition of great blessings. This I know to be true: daily immersion in God's love has awakened me to the multitude of moments where God is present, moments I might have missed, had I not taken the time to till my inner soil and still my restless spirit. Undergirding my prayer journey is a freedom that I never before imagined possible.　　—R.H.

❧ *Making Time for Prayer* ❧

Each Christian needs half an hour of prayer each day, except when we are busy. . . . Then we need an hour.
　　　　—St. Frances de Sales, as quoted in *Armchair Mystic*

I smile every time I read the quote above because in fact we are all so busy. But I have found that only the regular practice of prayer can develop a lasting habit. A daily rhythm of twenty to forty-five minutes or so is perhaps an appropriate amount of time. It often seems as though the time isn't there, but perhaps it's more a matter of desire, discipline, commitment, even self-permission to sit and waste time with God. *If prayer is an expression of our relationship with God, finding the time to cultivate and dwell in that relationship is essential — especially if we're busy!*

Fr. Mark Thibodeaux makes a very helpful distinction in his book Armchair Mystic. *He distinguishes between a* prayer-ful person, *one that tunes into the sacred throughout the day, and a* person of prayer *as one who claims daily time set aside for God. A person of prayer plans the day around designated prayer time instead of the other way around. Fr. Mark points out that sensing God's presence throughout the day is indeed important, but it's not enough. We become a prayerful person only by first becoming a person of prayer.*

Most struggle with finding or, as I would like to say, claiming time each day for prayer. I recall an idea shared by Anne Ortlund in her book Disciplines of the Beautiful Woman *that stayed with me for many years. As I remember, she spoke of her struggle with finding the time for prayer in her busy day, so she agreed to set her alarm in the middle of the night in order to have quality prayer time. In exchange for her commitment to God, she requested that God give her the energy for her daily family life. Her life was never the same. Mine wasn't either after reading her book. I never had an excuse again and often thought about Anne's fidelity during my own periodic bouts of insomnia. Considering it could be God's alarm going off, I would get up to pray instead of wallowing in sleeplessness.*

The following are some suggestions Lyn and I have found helpful:

- *Remember that prayer is a* grace, *a gift that we need to ask for. "Lord, teach me to pray" can be a great way to begin a prayer period.*

- *Pray for the grace of desire to commit yourself to a daily prayer routine. If you already have a routine, you might consider praying to see if you need to change it or extend your time.*

- *Choose a time of day when you are alert, but also when you find it easy to quiet yourself. For me, morning is the best, as it sets my day in a grace-filled manner.*

- *Eliminate distractions, phone, interruptions, etc.*

- *Choose a comfortable position and a warm, comforting setting. Candles, icons, photos, or spiritual pictures can be helpful aids. Have your Bible and journal near and handy, and perhaps even a meditation book as a source of inspiration.*

- *Start with short periods of time, perhaps five to ten minutes, and build up gradually.*

- *Choose one day a week when you are less scheduled and can devote more quality time to prayer. This will give your spirit more room to unwind and more time to surrender to the graces discovered in prayer.*

We have provided in this book information about various forms of prayer, and we hope that this will further assist you in creating your own prayer rhythms.

God, Why Do I Worry So Much?

And Peter answered him, "Lord, if it is you, bid me come to you on
the water."   —Matthew 14:28 NRSV

Sometimes little gusts of wind are more unbearable for the reed than
great storms.   —St. Thérèse of Lisieux

LHD It's been a tough week in subtle ways, I thought,
sitting at my large, cypress dining table sorting
through mail. While playing the keyboard for a funeral, I did
well until the Lamb of God and the Communion Song, both
of which I butchered. I looked in vain for the trapdoor that
my friend Bette Legendre says all musicians need to remove
themselves quickly from the scene. The next day, in a meeting
with two lovely women to plan an event, I felt tension and the
negative effects of unspoken frustrations that I felt I may have
caused. I immediately began to criticize myself internally and
I wished I had done things differently. Later in the week, I was
chatting with my husband, Dee, about some of his health issues, none of which are serious at this time. Subsequently and
unnecessarily, I descended into worry and fear as I thought,
"What would I ever do without him?" The rubbing and jousting
of everyday events seems to keep me stirred up.

In Matthew 14, we see the disciples trying to follow Jesus
and do his work. After the miracle of the loaves and the fishes

they are sent alone across the sea in their little boat. Their mountaintop experience is followed by separation and fear. The wind and waves begin to toss them, just as our lives toss us about, in large and small ways. Then, in the fourth watch of the night, they see Jesus coming to them over the waves! Peter, ever ready and impulsive, wants to be able to walk on the water too, but most of all, I think, he wants to end the separation between himself and his Beloved. He does well as long as he keeps his eyes on Jesus, but then fear overtakes him and he begins to sink.

Like the apostles in the boat I often feel separated from my Lord, from the big picture of what my life is to be, even after success and affirmation, especially after embarrassment and criticism. I become lost in irritations of my peace, fears that leave my soul feeling achy and raw.

Lost in thought this day, I opened my door and slowly walked into the front pasture, peering over the fence, into the trees, looking for my Beloved. Dappled sunlight and shade played in the narrow wooded area, and birds flitted easily among the bushes and trees and landed on the golden leaf carpet below. I pondered the state of my heart. It frightened me that so many things could upset my peace of mind. I considered the sensitivity and dependency that left me feeling so vulnerable, the need to please and to be special, to be good at everything. I knew that I was much more aware and more capable of coping with my inner life now than I used to be, but on this day it was not enough. I wanted to be free and mindless like the cardinals and sparrows that wafted through the trees.

Quickly another thought occurred: Was I really looking for God, or just for an easy way out of pain? Pain comes in many ways, large and small, and perhaps I wanted to walk on the water, to float over life with nary a rough spot or storm. Such a desire was not admirable, for in wanting this I turned away from the truth, truth that I think *does* lie in identifying my unnecessary suffering, my self-torture, the storms of my own creating.

I walked further, rounding the tree line, watching as a gray-brown rabbit darted away into hiding, showing me the flash of his snowy tail. I breathed, slowly, deeply. I cleared my mind and filled it with the blue sky. My heart reached to touch the unknown mystery, the hidden face. Peace trickled in and began to settle my stormy soul. I had been doing this form of quieting for quite a while now, and I did see some improvement in my character. I didn't run from my problems so quickly, I didn't rationalize my bad behavior away as much. I saw my part in creating problems more clearly, and yet I didn't seem to heap as much harsh retribution upon my own head. On the whole, my spirit had become more balanced and secure.

My friend Avis told me recently, "The prayer of quiet remolds our personalities. God's light shines in our dark corners and reveals us to ourselves. God's light heals." This prayer of quiet is to be willing to point ourselves in God's direction, to open ourselves to light rather than to achieve perfection on our own by a heroic effort. Little by little such a prayer charts a new course for our souls.

Then an unwelcome thought came to me, breaking into my fragile peace: "I will never arrive." I saw the subconscious fantasy that on some future day I would have struggled all I needed to, opened my heart all the way, done all that was necessary for growth, that I would sit easy in the armchair of knowing. I would achieve the enlightenment for which the Buddhists search, the attainment of the highest good on the spiritual path. This part of my road was veiled in deep mystery. It was enough; it should be enough for now, to be in the presence of God's light. I should not wish for the cessation of all present and future pain even if I admitted in a smaller part of myself I really did. Though pain teaches well, I could hope to learn in gentler ways, and as I walked I ardently wished for gentler ways.

As always, the weather was changing. A dark, misty, dragon-shaped cloud wove around the sun until the sun itself became smaller, a translucent dime in the sky. I considered how the disciples might have felt they had "arrived" when Jesus worked his mighty miracle and fed the hungry hoards. However, in no time at all, they were back in the sea, tossed around by nature and fear. Pain had arrived to teach its lesson: trust, and keep your eyes on Jesus. Let it be God's light that shines on in your hearts.

I took heart in the lives of seekers, such as the eloquent writer and monk Thomas Merton, a man whose writing testified to his immersion in God's love and grace. Yet Merton struggled with his own heart until his death, and I concluded that sometimes the most sincere of us struggle with ourselves all our lives. For some of us this incredibly sharp self-consciousness never seems to let us rest, and yet with time we learn better ways of coping and more awareness. We learn to practice trust in God. I know that I let go of my anger and negativity more quickly than I used to, and that for me this can become the active indifference that St. Ignatius of Loyola wrote about. But even the most sincere spiritual walk does not take away all our failings, our fears, and our suffering. Some may call this bad news, but I think it is also good news. Like that of the disciples, our inner growth doesn't stop; our lives need never stagnate or become lost in complacency. This adventure we call life will continue to challenge us until the end, and this keeps us fully alive.

Now, as I stood in the field and the light darkened, I enjoyed a cool breeze against my face. I pondered the things that battered me, like the winds of the Galilean storm. I moved from prayer to thinking and planning. I thought about whether I wanted to devote time to going to church and practicing the piano. (This practicing never seemed to happen; however, I was buying my sister-in-law's piano, and that was a hopeful sign.) I considered what I could have done differently before that meeting. Perhaps I communicated my inner thoughts somehow and they affected the atmosphere of the group. Cultivating blame seems to lead to hostile feelings inside and outside of us.

I resolved to be more aware of what I was thinking and to avoid future cultivation of blaming, negative thoughts.

I prayed for guidance about my husband's health. I realized that I went about my days mostly wrapped in the clouds of my own goals and activities. I knew he was sometimes lonely and that my busyness may have added to his stress.

I tried to practice self-forgiveness now, for I realized the truth of what Rabbi Harold Kushner wrote: "The illusion that we can control events if we do everything right, make people love us and guarantee happy endings, is just that . . . an illusion."

As I let go, my peace of heart was deepened. Thank you, God. The prayer of quiet had provided access to a river of flowing awareness and courage within me.

I asked for God's wisdom. I took courage in God's love, and I tried to keep my eyes on Jesus. I considered the birds of the field, the stunning red of the cardinal that flashed in the gathering dusk; he was dressed by God alone. Tiny white flowers that neither reaped nor sowed were drifting about my feet. "Let things go," I said to myself. "Trust. Let God do God's work in you."

Our daily struggles will continue, for we can cultivate only that ground on which we stand. As Peter might have said, we sail where our boat is, sometimes tossed by storms, sometimes navigating smoothly, but always with hope as our companion.   —L.H.D.

⤳ *Centering Prayer* ⤶

Centering Prayer can be done either sitting or walking, but you may want to begin to practice it in the sitting position.

Before beginning, ask God to come into your prayer of quiet and be with you.

Sit quietly and comfortably in a position that does not lull you into sleep. Tune into your breathing and note the in and out of it. Begin to breathe more slowly and smoothly. In general I breathe in through my nose and out through my mouth. I like to prolong the exhale somewhat, blowing it gently out of my mouth. To begin, you may put your hands on your diaphragm, just above and below the belt line. This area should expand outward gently on the inhale and retract on the ex-hale. If you begin to feel your breath in your whole body, this is good.

As you still yourself, you will quickly become aware of your mind chatter, of many thoughts appearing, worries and tasks demanding your attention. Just watch your thoughts, as you would disinterestedly watch clouds in the sky. Don't try to dispel the thoughts. Don't engage them.

You may employ a word that you say silently every few sec-onds such as "Jesus" or "love." I like to use the letter/symbol, "O." This letter connotes wholeness to me, yet allows me to stay in a nonthinking mode. I visualize "O" on my exhale. I also see my mind as a blank or as a soft color, like light blue.

Feel yourself descend into quiet as you center in this prayer. If you allow it, after some repetition, quiet will fill your soul.

This prayer can be used alone to quiet the heart, or it can be a gateway to many other forms of prayer, some of which are described in this book.

God, Use Me

I waited, waited for the LORD; who bent down and heard my cry,
Drew me out of the pit of destruction,
out of the mud of the swamp,
Set my feet upon rock, steadied my steps,
And put a new song in my mouth, a hymn to our God.
Many shall look on in awe and they shall trust in the LORD.
— Psalm 40:1–4 NAB

When you're waiting, you're *not* doing nothing. You're doing the most important something there is. You're allowing your soul to grow up.　　　　　　　— Sue Monk Kidd, *When the Heart Waits*

RH In the fall of 1990, my world turned upside down. Married for fifteen years, I was thirty-seven years old and the mother of four, ages thirteen, eleven, nine, and seven. Tension had wrapped around our home like a rubber band stretched to its limits. My husband and I were both hurting, and, locked into our customary unhealthy behaviors, he fled and I tried to fix. The forsaken day arrived, however, when the inevitable occurred: the band snapped, and our marriage ended.

Those first weeks after he left, I could hardly breathe through the fear and hurt that had imprisoned my heart. Just getting the kids dressed and off to school was an ordeal. My pain overtook every cell of my spirit, and I cried off and on every day. Being in public felt like walking around town with a scarlet letter on my chest. I could even picture it as a bold black S. It stood for "Separated." My emotional outbursts were frequent, and I found myself embarrassed and ashamed most of the time. Seeing other intact families was painful, so I opted to stay home as much as I could. Friends brought meals, offered to take my turn for carpool, and lent listening ears. In many ways, those days were sacred and filled with tender care. I was blessed by concerned and loving family and friends and by an internal strength I never knew existed.

Not long after the separation, my eleven-year-old son, Ryan, excitedly came home from school with the announcement that he had been chosen to be an altar server for the annual bishop's Mass. Bishop Flynn made it a point each year to visit every Catholic school in the diocese, and that Friday would be our turn. I dreaded being in public, but I would not have missed the holy event for anything in the world.

That Friday morning, I noticed Ryan had gotten up extra early to blow-dry his hair, and it lifted my spirits to see his enthusiasm. I felt a strange sense of peace in recognizing that it was no accident he'd been chosen for the honorable role, drawing me out of the isolation to which I'd become accustomed during the past few weeks.

Sitting in church with my mom and my two younger children, I felt strengthened by the appearance of the bishop as he processed up the aisle. I recalled a previous encounter when he and I seemed to lock glances as he approached that same space. I had felt a deep connection to his contemplative presence, a warm tingling from head to toe. I became aware of the identical feeling rising up in me at that moment. In his presence, I could hear an echo of Julian of Norwich's famous words, "And all shall be well."

As Bishop Flynn got closer to where we were sitting, I noticed that he was donning the vestment my son Michael's kindergarten class had made for our pastor the previous year. It was brightly decorated with little handprints, finger-painted in primary colors, covering the white garment. I smiled inside seeing him wear it and overheard Michael lean over to his grandmother and whisper proudly, "Mine is the green one right in the front!"

Mass was always so special when Bishop Flynn presided, because he had a loving way with the children that was so endearing. At the end of that Mass, he did something I'd seen him do on other occasions: acknowledge *anyone* who had *anything* to do with the Mass. I observed Ryan smiling proudly, straightening up taller as he listened to what a good job he had done. The teachers, the choir, the readers, even the 850 students got thanked. At the end of the litany of acknowledgments, my ears perked up. Bishop Flynn stood in the center of the altar, lifted his arms wide, and glanced down at the vestment. I felt an odd sense of knowing what was coming next. Smiling, he teasingly asked the children, "But what I want to know is, whose handprint is this?" pointing to *the green one right in the front*. Michael shot out of the pew waving his hand wildly. My heart melted. Those little hands seemed to be holding me together.

When my nine-year-old, Emily, asked after Mass if she could get her new First Communion rosary blessed by the bishop, I knew the forces of good were working to put me in his path. We caught him right outside of church, and I sensed the distinct urge to seek him privately for prayers.

I noticed that his car was blocked in, so without hesitation, I dashed to his side before the obstructing car could be moved. I approached him with hope in my heart that prayers from this elevated soul would restore my marriage. I have no recollection to this day of what I told him, only the gush of tears and emotion that poured forth. What I will *never* forget was the look of love and compassion on his face and the words that followed: "Have courage. Have courage. I will pray for you, Robin, but you must have courage." I felt saturated by grace and knew in my heart that this encounter would be only the beginning of what this man would give me in my life.

IN THE MONTHS that followed, "Have courage" translated into having courage to grieve. I had to face my utter vulnerability and discover that I was not in control of my life, something about which I had always deceived myself. Learning firsthand that I couldn't fix, clutch, or demand was a grueling lesson. It was especially painful to begin to face the mistakes I had made along the way in my marriage and to make amends, mostly to myself. Many mornings I would sit in my bedroom chair and sob with one eye on the clock. I would pat my face with water and then rush off to work. The words "This is a nervous breakdown" would haunt my mind.

That first year was challenging in every way — certainly financially, but mostly emotionally and spiritually. God was someone I prayed to, but I saw him more as a taskmaster than a confidant. He wasn't answering my desperate plea, or my trusted bishop's prayers, to bring my husband home and my family back together. I never gave up praying, but I lacked a relationship that could sustain and strengthen my torn spirit. I was losing my footing and seemed to sink deeper into despair and anger.

One night as I lay in bed crying, Emily was lying next to me. Noticing a forlorn look on her face, I asked her what she was thinking. Her response rattled me to my core. She spoke sadly, "I'm wondering what it'll be like to have a mother that cries for the rest of my life."

Strength is a funny thing. We think it's something we can self-generate. But I've discovered it's a grace, given to us when we surrender our own will to divine care and wisdom. True, we're strongest when we're weakest, but even so, gaining strength by acknowledging our weakness is much easier said than done.

During that period, I uncovered the courage to slow down and cut some of the nonessentials out of my life, which gave me time to face myself. I found that I was suspended in mid-air, not going forward or backward, that awkward in-between stage that caterpillars know so very well. The Israelites in the desert knew this in-between time, as did Jesus in the tomb, at least for a few days. I've always said that as Christians, the Paschal mystery supplies our hope, but those Holy Saturdays can be awfully long. T. S. Eliot's words in the *Four Quartets* became my mantra: "I said to my soul, be still, and wait without hope, for hope would be hope for the wrong thing."

To assist in this cocoon period my friend Ellen gave me a book that would cradle me in my discomfort and become a beacon of light, even though its illumination was so very far off in the distance. As I read it, Sue Monk Kidd's *When the Heart Waits*, I experienced a new concept of waiting, that of a sacrament. Sue sees waiting as the missing link in our spiritual evolution, a lost, forgotten experience crucial to becoming fully human, fully

Christian, fully ourselves. Her own midlife journey described in her book gave meaning to my own, and in reading her story we became soul sisters. I held on to her words, her hope, her resurrection.

In the years that followed, it took courage to be open to community and to risk sharing my pain with others. It took courage to go deeper in my prayer life, to pray for the grace to let go and to trust that God can do a whole lot better job with my life than I can. And finally, it took enormous courage to embrace these words heard on a Paula D'Arcy retreat: "Your journey begins when you give up expecting your life to turn out a certain way." Her message gave me permission to walk a new path.

Now I see how the journey I traveled was part of a larger plan for my life, that the prayer of my pain was meant to change me, not my circumstances. Looking back on the events of that day at the children's Mass and the multitude of blessings that have followed, I am struck with wonder by the presence of God holding me up in even my darkest hour.

COURAGE ALSO BROUGHT ME BACK to Bishop Flynn and put me again in his care. Strengthened by the healing that was beginning to take place, I found myself stepping out a bit and saying yes to new challenges. One of those was to Theresians, the Catholic ministry of women I'd been involved with for many years. These had been the women who had provided such a healing space in my darkest times. Now it was my turn to give back. Named as national president, I was panicked over the responsibility and realized in an inspired moment that my beloved friend was our national episcopal advisor, Bishop Flynn, who always loved Theresians and was quite open when I called him for spiritual direction.

Even though it had occurred years before, he hadn't forgotten our initial meeting in the church parking lot and welcomed me with open arms. The first time I entered his stately office was like a half-hour ticket to heaven. I could breathe in the peace. Tears streamed down my cheeks, but not tears of sadness as they once were. These tears hailed an awareness I've come to know many times since, a feeling of total immersion in God's presence. His opening words were profound and quite challenging: "It is clear you have been sanctified by your pain. Now your prayer must be 'God use me. You use me, God.' You must pray that every day, Robin." Those words became my personal fiat.

When our Blessed Mother uttered her own fiat, "Be it done to me according to thy word," I can only imagine that she spoke with fear and hesitation. To be used by God is a total surrender of self. It took me a long time before I could speak those words and truly mean them. There are still days when I struggle to trust God that much.

Through the three private sessions I had with him, Bishop Flynn taught me so very much about prayer. "God is a jealous lover," he instructed. "He wants your attention. Unless you're growing in union, being in his presence, allowing him to transform you, you're running around in circles."

He would remind me at each meeting that I was called to a deep, deep union with God and must stand alone before him. Although it took me years to begin to comprehend the profundity of his message, through his loving direction that year, I began to find the courage for more silence and solitude, something I had unknowingly avoided. My journey clearly took on new depths, and God gradually became someone whose arms I wanted to crawl into.

Most recently, I discovered that my spiritual companion, now archbishop of St. Paul/Minneapolis, would be back in Lafayette, saying Mass at the Cathedral of St. John. I longed to recapture that same transcendent feeling I'd experienced in his office over nine years ago. As I sat in the pew amid the newly renovated walls and ceilings of the splendid cathedral, the discovery dawned that I, too, had changed. It felt uplifting to be in the archbishop's presence and to feel his strength without *needing* it. The holiness I'd sought in and through him was within myself all along. Both the cathedral and I had been restored to our original beauty.

Stepping into the receiving line after Mass, I was elated to have the chance to speak a few personal words to my old friend. It stunned me that before I could open my mouth to reintroduce myself, he was already speaking my name. Bending to reach my short stature, he surprised me with the most tender words: "There was one thing I never understood, Robin. It was why you had to suffer all that pain." As I walked away, I felt like I had come full circle, to a place of wholeness for which I had longed those many years ago. I knew the answer to his question, even if he didn't remember speaking these words to me so many years ago: "For when the well runs dry, that's when love is learned and the capacity for God is vast." —R.H.

～ A Special Community of Women ～

Theresians is a contemporary Catholic/Christian organization for women providing a global network of small faith communities. Theresians was founded in 1961 in Pueblo, Colorado, by Msgr. Elwood Voss, who felt that there was little contemporary inspiration for women in the Catholic Church. Voss saw that "women were accustomed to giving of themselves in church and society, but were not often provided with in-depth opportunities for self-enrichment and spiritual growth. His solution was an organization that would provide women with an opportunity to enrich their own lives through spiritual development, ongoing education, affirmation and encouragement in their vocations, a deep community experience, and a ministry to others."

Theresian women are committed to a way of life *that integrates five dimensions: spirituality, education, vocation, community, and ministry. Within small faith communities, from twelve to twenty women in each group, Theresians pledge support by prayerfully nurturing, affirming, and empowering each other to become the women God intends them to be. Members meet monthly in one another's homes to study, pray, and break bread together. But far from being serious study sessions, these meetings are experiences of joyful and sharing community.*

My own twenty-year journey with my "Open Heart" community, as well as my connection to Theresian women around the country and the world, has provided the spiritual touchstone in my life from which my entire journey has evolved. Lyn says of her experience with Theresians, "Women I knew all my life became true heart's friends during our Theresian walk. We have laughed, sung, played, prayed, birthed, and cried together in a unique sacred community of belonging."

For further information about Theresians visit their website at www.Theresians.org.

I Am Filled with Your Light

Six days later, Jesus took with him Peter and James and his brother
John and led them up a high mountain, by themselves. And he was
transfigured before them, and his face shone like the sun, and his
clothes became dazzling white. — Matthew 17:1–2 NRSV

...that they may all be one. As you, Father, are in me and I am in
you, may they also be in us, so that the world may believe that you
have sent me. The glory that you have given me I have given them,
so that they may be one, as we are one, I in them and you in me, that
they may become completely one, so that the world may know that
you have sent me and have loved them even as you have loved me.
— John 17:21–23 NRSV

LHD I sat on a swing in a big pasture in Grand Coteau,
Louisiana, on a clear and sunny day during a retreat
that I was helping to direct. I always felt different in this pasture; I felt close to heaven. It was a place that evoked deeply
peaceful memories within me.

Now, during a break in my schedule I pondered the Gospel
words concerning the Transfiguration of Christ, a biblical event
that had always captivated me. I once heard in a homily that
the light within Jesus that shone so brightly on that day was
always present within him. It was not normally seen by the
disciples. Perhaps they were different on that day as well, more
open to God's light. I mused about God being light within and
around us.

I thumbed through the book *Light from Light* and found these phrases: "The soul responds to a mysterious desire for God in a love that surpasses our knowledge of God." The authors further explain that this dark knowledge of God becomes the soul's only light and that this light of love is "blinding" and "incomprehensible" to our ordinary vision. A sweet recognition stirred within me as I read, something deeper than the words themselves.

We can all, perhaps, recount certain moments in our lives when hidden light was present to our souls, when the veil between heaven and earth grew thin, when we saw mystery. We were suddenly struck by the light on the leaves, the red of a sunset, the yearning in our prayer. God spoke to us in falling water and hushed breeze, in salty earth and endless sky. We were touched by we knew not what. We stood suddenly in the light. We were one with it. We were filled with it. We wanted to stay with it forever. The words of Jesus in the Gospel of John quoted above became fulfilled within our very lives, as all pain dissolved in unity. I have read of many such experiences, and I have written of special ones that I myself have had. Now, thinking of such moments, I scribbled shapes in my journal, drawing nothing at all.

Suddenly, the clear remembrance of another personal transfiguration came to me as I swayed in the wooden swing, my journal on my lap, the sun warming my shoulders. It had happened years ago, during the stressful years when I was a teacher and my husband and I were raising our little son. The memory came back clearly, in one lovely piece.

I WAS DRIVING in an unfamiliar part of the village where I lived close to the river; trees were everywhere. Classical music was on the radio, violins played, many strings; the music was piercingly beautiful.

Suddenly, time stopped. As I looked out the windshield, I saw that everything was suffused in golden light, but not the light of the sun, or anything familiar. It was my inner light, or it was God's light, projected, a gauzy radiance that wrapped around everything, transforming individual things into a sacred whole. Everything had always been present and would always be present, as eternal energy, a manifestation of love. The whole world was glowing and eternal, and there was a dreamlike quality, but this was not a dream. I was transfixed, even as I continued to drive.

I received this message, silently, in my heart: "All is one. Nothing dies. All is one. There is no separation... all is one ... all is one." The experience lasted a few minutes and was timeless. Trees, plants, earth, people, everything as *one*. An ancient knowing, revealed to me. God manifested in this world. So beautiful!

I stirred in the swing in the Grand Coteau pasture. I hadn't thought of this experience in so long! Why had this happened to me? I couldn't think of anything I had done to precipitate or deserve this illumination. As I pondered it, it seemed a stunning grace. Perhaps I had been learning at that time to cultivate a new awareness. Still, I felt that this experience had been pure gift.

I left the swing and walked to my retreat office. During the next two hours I listened to the dear women on retreat, one by one. I struggled to be some sort of container for their brokenness. Husbands cold and distant, husbands cruel. Children now gone from the earth, children lost to drugs, children... lost.

Grinding work for which others took credit. Weariness, depression, and illness. Beloved spouses now gone. Loneliness deep and festering. I listened. I struggled. I was totally inadequate. I gently called them to prayer; I told them, "God loves you."

During my private prayer that followed, I lifted them to God. I visualized each of them surrounded by the same golden light that I saw on that long-ago day. I saw them transfigured. I prayed for them and for me with deep feeling, "Let us be one in you, Jesus, as you and the Father are one."

When the day ended, I retired and slept soundly. I rose at 6:30, longing for coffee. I slipped on clothes and walked outside to the courtyard. As I took a few steps forward, I stopped, stunned. On the far side of the courtyard, above the graceful steppings of the soft yellow façade, the light was streaming, up and up. Apricot, peach, ruby-red, and burnt orange rays were shooting into the sky, as brilliant as fireworks, as gentle as mist, and over all was suffused a liquid golden light. I stood and gazed, transfixed. "I am always missing this," I thought. "It is always here, and I miss it." The light entered and warmed me, vibrated within me.

Later, I sipped my coffee and tried to put it all together. I was left with mystery. I would never understand all the brokenness in our world, the suffering, for example, of twenty-six good women on a retreat in Grand Coteau in the summer of 2003. Yet, somehow, for one day, my heart was transfigured. A light not normally visible had visited my memory, my vision. The cloud of unknowing-darkness within me was illuminated, infusing knowledge into some oft hidden part of my soul. I was one with the wise, eternal, and graced part of me that knew fully, All is one and all is well. —L.H.D.

Sitting Here with You

The priorities of prayer and hospitality are rooted in the *Rule of St. Benedict*, a foundation that lies behind most monastic life today. Benedict's balanced view of life calls monks and sisters to a rhythm and order that are visible when visiting a monastery.... Many people at midlife have talked with me about the ways they have been impacted by visits to monasteries. They have enjoyed the quiet and reflection while they are there, and they have also carried something significant back home with them.

—Lynne Baab, *A Renewed Spirituality*

RH One of my favorite memories of prayer involves an aged little nun, a tiny Benedictine sister who lived at the Benet Hill Monastery in the aspen-laden woods of Colorado Springs. I loved her name: *Maristelle*. It means "Star of the Sea." She recently died, but our very brief friendship made a lasting impression on my soul.

When I visited her monastery, I was on business in a way, taking time apart to work on an agenda for an upcoming meeting. Looking forward to my planning time while nestled in the midst of the Rocky Mountains, I hoped to live it in balance in the true style of St. Benedict.

Every time I saw Sr. Maristelle, she showed me the comforting spirit of Benedictine hospitality, inquiring how my work was coming along and then sweetly marking my forehead with the sign of the cross, adding the words, "May Jesus bless you, my friend." Hunched over, she could hardly reach my forehead even though I'm only five feet tall. But I could always catch a glimpse of the love in her sparkling eyes. On one such occasion, her mark of holiness accomplished its work of keeping my mind focused. I found myself moved to ask if I could join her when she prayed.

I reverently entered the chapel early the next morning, not knowing what to expect, but anticipating a heightened awareness of God's presence. As I glanced toward the massive picture window, a vision of Pike's Peak in its exquisite splendor filled the holy space, an image of God's grandeur. How easy it was to feel his presence here! I glanced around the sacred space and could sense the energy of deeply felt prayers and holiness. I expected that the entire community of sisters would be gathered, but instead there was only Sr. Maristelle, waiting silently near a little round table. It was as if I had been granted an invitation to her private cloister.

On top of the table were two objects, a small candle and an ordinary kitchen timer. Sister motioned to me to sit on the tiny stool near the table. She lit the candle, adjusted the timer, and then leaned over to me and whispered, "Now, little Robin, we're going to sit here and let God love us for twenty minutes."

For the first time in my life, I was able to allow God to free my spirit completely so he could fill me from head to toe with his very own. My body felt as light as a feather. I seemed to float to another dimension in time and space. Buoyed by the holiness of my prayer partner and the sacred space she helped create, my cluttered mind relaxed and the burdensome thoughts that always weigh me down during prayer time passed away like drifting clouds. My state of being felt pure and weightless, free of the past and future.

Those privileged moments of shared prayer offered an experience of union — with God, with another's heart, with the

Benedictine sisters at the monastery, with the yearning of all who share the deepest desire in our souls for God. When the little timer rang, I had to pull myself back from heaven. I could hardly believe that twenty minutes had just transpired. I discovered that morning that prayer is not something to be learned, but a desire to be shared, experienced, lived.

Often when I sit for my daily centering prayer time, I hear an echo of Sr. Maristelle's priceless words in my heart and thank God for loving me — not just for twenty minutes but for an eternity. — R.H.

God, I Did It Again!

We have to train ourselves to see how we give an "effective charge" to the offense, how we are getting energy from mulling over someone else's mistakes. We can build a case with no effort at all.... The verdict is in: the other person is guilty. And wrong besides. And because the other is wrong, we are right.... Only the contemplative mind can recognize its own participation and complicity in this great mystery of evil.
— Richard Rohr, *Everything Belongs*

LHD My husband and I went with our friends the Arnolds to Florida one spring, but Mac Arnold doesn't really like to travel. He likes to be at his camp on the Atchafalaya River. In fact when he is not at his camp, he is not really happy.

Now his wife and I knew this about him, but always hopeful, we two couples planned a vacation that included days on the beach and a trip to Animal Kingdom at Disney World.

True to form, Mac absolutely refused to be entertained and constantly said he was bored. The final straw for me came after the tour at Animal Kingdom, during which we saw every African animal imaginable, all in natural-looking habitats, including a beautiful white rhino.

At this point Mac announced, "I wouldn't have gone across the street to see that."

I picked up *The Florida Tourist Magazine* and beat him across the head, at first playfully, but then furiously. He finally thrust the magazine away and looked at me in amazement.

What was this? What shadow had I turned up within myself?

In my books and my talks I often speak of detachment from another's behavior, stating that the only person one can control is one's self. I am better at expressing these principles than living them out, proved by the fact that I hit people on the head with magazines when they upset or disappoint me.

The next day, the four of us went to the Strawberry Festival and waded through large crowds to sample various strawberry desserts and look at farm animals. (Maybe this *was* a boring vacation.) A curious thing happened there. A woman walked up to me and pressed a metallic sticker onto my shirt, then turned and disappeared into the crowd. The sticker read, "John 4:4." John 4:4? I would have expected John 3:16, "For God so loved the world that he gave his only begotten son. . . . " But why John 4:4? I took it off my shirt and it found its way into my purse, where it stuck on the inside. I saw it every time I went into my purse.

The next morning, I took the sticker, my notebook, and Bible out to the beach. I had recognized the Scripture passage on the sticker. It was the story of Jesus' encounter with the Samaritan woman at Jacob's well, where he offers her living water, so that she may never thirst again.

I read verse 4: "He had to pass through Samaria."

At the time, I couldn't think of how it might apply to my situation, and yet, I thought, there must be a reason this Scripture passage is being put in front of me. In my journal I wrote, "I realize, Lord, how in judgment I am of myself and others. I want still (!) to control the thoughts and feelings of those around me. Why must I be triggered by the fact that Mac is bored? Why does this bother me? Why do I waste my peace and my energy? If it were just Mac and just a vacation, it wouldn't matter so much, God. But I think this behavior spills over into much of my life. Even when I don't say anything, I am sizing people up, criticizing."

I wondered if this was a fight that I would ever win.

The cool beach wind blew across my face, my neck, and my arms. An old man wearing a black elastic bandage around his knee walked slowly down the beach and lifted his hand to me in greeting. He was limping, yet he walked. It must have been painful, but on he walked.

I read the fourth chapter of John again and then reread the fourth verse, which explained that Jesus *had* to go through Samaria. I closed my eyes and went into centering prayer. Slowly, I imagined the dusty scene, the woman beside the well. I became present there; I stood in the shadow of the well, unseen, as Jesus approached. I watched as he spoke to her, and I saw her distrust turn to joy. She ran into the village to tell everyone that she had met someone who redeemed her life and filled her thirsty heart.

In my imagination, I approached Jesus from the shadows. I said to him, "Master, did you *have* to go through Samaria?"

"Of course I did. She was waiting for me."

I didn't engage in the exercise of saying that she wasn't waiting, that she didn't know him. Obviously, she had been waiting for him all her life.

"Jesus," I said, "you gave her living water and told her all that she needed to know to live fully. What do you have to tell me?"

My imagination soared as he looked at me kindly for a long moment, his eyes twinkling. "You are made in God's image, sweet daughter, but you know, you are not God."

Whoa! I opened my eyes and returned to the present, surprised and filled to the brim with the depth and reality of my experience. The sage-green waves rolled onto the beach, where brightly clad children were dancing about as mothers and fathers spread out towels and put up umbrellas. The seagulls swooped and the crushed-pecan sand was warm beneath my feet.

I took up my journal again and wrote: "I often express that I want to love others more. I see how this love is constantly marred by my worry about what others think of me and my own hard thoughts about them. I am carrying too much baggage. My judging mind gives me no peace. My shadows engulf me and make me sick of myself! I have been trying so hard, when I just need to receive. I see now that my job is to let go of as much as I can or else my hands will be much too full to receive your living water. Especially if I try to be God instead of being just me, your sweet daughter."

Putting my pen down, I remembered that Jesus, who was God, came empty-handed to the encounter in Samaria, the shadowland, home of Jewish projections of evil spirits, curses, and people who were only half human in Hebrew eyes. Rejecting these false perceptions Jesus had to go to this dark place to redeem what was lost and so did I. As the children's song "Going on a Bear Hunt" says, "Can't go over it, can't go under it. Gotta go through it." And if I didn't go through my shadowland I would have been there permanently, lost in the falseness of my very self, powered by an ego that seeks to be God.*

The woman of Samaria was filled with *her* judgments. She knew how one must draw water and to whom one could speak. And yet she was forced to leave all this behind, just as I now struggled to redeem the harshness of my small mind. She even had to release her hard thoughts about herself, as she lived the words of Isaiah: "You will draw water joyfully, from the springs of salvation."

It was much easier to apologize to Mac after my encounter with Jesus on a Florida beach beside the well of living water, though I didn't do it perfectly. I said, "Mac, I guess I was really hoping you would enjoy this vacation and I was disappointed, but that's no excuse for beating you over the head with a magazine. I apologize." I see now how I was still justifying my actions. Mac had disappointed me, but it was reconciliation after all.

"Did you hit me on the head with a magazine?" he asked, rubbing his temple. We both chuckled about it. Mac's probably not going to change his attitudes, but I can change my own.

The John 4:4 sticker stayed on the inside of my purse for a long time. It called me away from my chattering mind (which always claims to know so much). It called me into the mystery of spirit and the joy of salvation. There, living water quenches thirst; shadows give way to light, and love is so much bigger than I am.   —L.H.D.

---

*In *Mystical Christianity: A Psychological Commentary on the Gospel of John,* John Sanford tells us that the water Christ offers "is the healing water that comes up from within. It heals the weary ego and refreshes the soul." This water is the water of Wisdom. Sanford states that "the most important place where the Word of God was to be found for the early Christians was in the soul herself, where it lived as *imago dei, like a spring of water from which flowed the knowledge of God."* Emphasis added.

∽ *Praying with Scripture* ∾ *and Imagination*

My prayer experiences with Scripture have been deeply enriched by using imaginative visualization. I perceive this form of devotion as a keystone of Ignatian prayer experiences.

This method came easily to me, as I was always a dreamy girl, lost in my fantasies. I have put myself to sleep for many years by spinning tales in which I am the hero.

Using imagination with Scripture is different and more important, of course, but it builds on these very day-dreaming skills. In addition we are relying on the Holy Spirit to come to us and help bring images to us. This type of imaginative prayer lifts the Bible characters off the page and makes them come alive! It also opens our hearts in a new way to Jesus' message. Here are some steps to follow:

1. *Pick a story from one of the Gospels. I have listed some suggestions below.*

2. *Light a candle, quiet your heart with gentle breathing, and say an opening prayer such as the following: Dear God, Holy Spirit, as I pray with your sacred word today, open my spirit to its message. Make your Scripture real in my heart. Teach me what you would have me learn and fill me with your knowledge and your love. Amen.*

3. *Read the Gospel passage slowly and prayerfully, noticing the movements of your heart.*

4. *Read the story again and begin to visualize the place and the people as well as the action of the story. For example,*

*is the day dusty and hot? Are people eager, angry, or joy-
ful? What colors do you see? Who captures your attention
in the story? What are the high points in the action of the
story? How would you have fit into the action if you had
lived in that day?*

5. *Now close your eyes and clearly visualize the scene again.
   Put yourself in the story. You can be one of the main
   characters, an onlooker, a servant, or whoever you wish
   to be. See everything in your imagination as clearly as you
   can and follow the story to its ending. Here's a tricky part:
   try not to overcontrol your experience. Surprising things
   may start to happen; release your preconceived notions
   and flow in the river of the prayer.*

6. *In your imagination how are you responding to Jesus and
   to others? Do you talk to anyone? For example, when I
   entered the scene of Jesus' birth in a deep prayer experience I was able to talk with Joseph, learning much about
   the state of his heart, his worries and his love for Mary. I
   have loved Joseph more deeply ever since that experience.
   Note what you are feeling, as your feeling state is very important in this process, but don't strain to feel anything
   in particular.*

7. *Journal about your experience in as much depth as you
   can, reflecting on the gifts of this prayer session.*

8. *Suggested Closing Prayer: Holy Spirit, thank you for coming to be with me today in my prayer. I love you and
   I know that your being enlivens Holy Scripture. Jesus,
   thank you for the privilege of walking with you and
   learning to love you more. Amen.*

Suggested Gospel Passages for Imaginative Prayer

The subheads for the following Gospel passages come from the New American Bible. However, use any translation that you are comfortable with.

Luke 7:11–17	The Raising of the Widow's Son
Luke 7:36–50	The Pardon of the Sinful Woman
Luke 10:38–42	Martha and Mary
Mark 5:25–34	The Woman with a Hemorrhage
Mark 10:17–22	The Rich Young Man
Matthew 15:21–28	The Canaanite Woman's Faith
John 4:4–42	The Samaritan Woman
John 5:1–18	Cure on a Sabbath

There are numerous other passages that you will enjoy using in this form of prayer. Look for passages in which Jesus is engaged in the active life of his ministry, whether healing, teaching, or showing his unconditional love to others. Let your imagination soar.

You, Alone, Are Enough

Jesus is happy to show me the only path to the divine blazing fire. This path is the self-abandonment of the little child who sleeps without fear in his father's arms.

—St. Thérèse of Lisieux: General Correspondence

For I know well the plans I have in mind for you, says the Lord, plans for your welfare, not for woe! plans to give you a future full of hope. When you call me, when you go to pray to me, I will listen to you. When you look for me, you will find me. Yes, when you seek me with all your heart, you will find me with you, says the Lord, and I will change your lot. *— Jeremiah 29:11–14a NAB*

RH I have had the humble privilege of traveling on several occasions as a missionary to a very poor village in northeast Mexico. Every time I have gone, I have witnessed in myself a great resistance that bubbles up just weeks before the trip, as if each mission offers me an occasion to purge whatever is currently blocking my inner freedom. Before one such visit, it took everything in me to simply pack and show up for the Mass that would see us off on our journey. The very morning of our departure, I had suffered a heartbreaking rejection, projecting me into a tailspin regarding my future. God's apparent invitation to submit my life to him seemed a tall order for me to accept.

My initial resistance usually disappears as I step foot in the travel vehicle, but on that particular trip, it took days for me to let go. My inner whining was repulsive even to myself. I couldn't release my troubles back home, especially at night when, instead of sleeping, I was obsessing about my hurt and disgusted with how much focus was on myself. Praying desperately for openness, I turned to St. Thérèse of Lisieux, Patroness of Missionaries, for intercession since, I felt, she had drawn me into this kind of work in the first place.

On the fourth morning, after days of self-preoccupation and yet another sleepless night, I was preparing to return to our assigned work site when I distinctly heard the words "Give me this day."

"What do you mean, Lord?" I responded.

I was looking forward to getting back to my job as "mud maker" for the adobe bricks used for the house we'd been building, since the work distracted me from my fears and pain. Indeed, my efforts in the mud pile had been the saving grace those last few days, as it was the only place where I was feeling productive, useful, and other-centered. In addition, our Nigerian associate pastor, Fr. Isaac Opara, provided relief and joy with his resounding laughter that seemed to take the edge off of our hard work and my troubled spirit. If I didn't go back to work that day, I would miss all of that. I listened more deeply, began to cry, and wrote in my journal: "Sometimes my prayer-time tears are about joy. Sometimes sadness. And like today God uses them to simply break open my heart to let him in more fully." I could feel trust beginning to envelop me.

In response, God whispered, "Let me have you this day. Let's have a quiet day together. Just you and me." I yearned for his comfort and willingly responded.

Knowing it was the first time I had surrendered since I'd left home, I decided to speak with the mission leader about my intent to stay back that day, and with my journal I climbed the concrete stairs to that one place in my world that I hold most sacred. The chapel at the casa is a small consecrated space in which I have experienced many blessed moments over the years, often praying on the Saltillo-tiled floor right at daybreak as the sun rises over the trees, visible through the little square windows.

Arriving in my sacred refuge, I was drawn to lie down on the colorful striped pillows lining the far wall, and there I fell into the most restful sleep I'd had in months. I could feel Jesus' arms surrounding me, enveloping me like a tiny child, and in my slumber I could vaguely hear the echoes of the children playing downstairs and the hum of the tiny washing machine that labored day and night. The smell of beans simmering in the kitchen filtered through the open windows of my tiny piece of heaven on earth. The familiar sounds of the burros as well as the Mexican music in the distance provided the comfort of knowing I was in my beloved space. The warm air transported me to the pre-air-conditioned, carefree days of my childhood. On awakening, I had a deep sense of peace and restoration and the distinct feeling that I was being prepared for something.

Then in my heart I heard the words "Get a book and read." I quickly thought of the reading material I'd brought with me and knew that none of it was what I needed. I considered searching around the house for something, but at that moment my eyes were drawn to the floor. I had not noticed the little book lying only a few feet away. Reaching for it, I knew by the feeling of aliveness inside of me that this was no ordinary moment and that this was not an ordinary book. It was Thomas à Kempis's *The Imitation of Christ,* which I had seen quoted on occasion but had never read. I opened the book somewhere in the middle, and the first words I read graced my longing spirit with openness and trust: "Be silent and endure for a while and you will experience the help of God in your need. No doubt, for God knows when and how to deliver you. So put yourself in his care."

Every word I read seemed to strike a chord deep within, and within minutes I was feverishly jotting line after line in my journal, stunned over the seeming coincidences of my personal issues and the holy advice being offered. Every theme in my life appeared to be addressed: facing honestly my selfish tendencies and possessive nature, emptying my heart of excessive desires, and seeking the strength to trust God completely, humbly relying on his grace alone. I wept in awe. I felt lifted into a space where God was so real, where he was filling me with his truth, as if he were sitting there with me teaching me about my sinfulness. It was a loving reproach, and I was ready for healing and reconciliation. I had never in my life felt so close, so intimate, so cherished by my Father. If only for a priceless segment of time, God alone was enough.

I read and wrote for four hours. Pondering the themes of humility, littleness, and confidence in God in my reading, I began to see in this little treasure of a book hints of the spirituality of St. Thérèse. I started to wonder about any connection she might have had to this text, since her fingerprints seemed to be all over my experience that day. She had always seen her own littleness not as an obstacle, but as an asset in accepting God's mercy. I felt as though my own *littleness* was in fact being transformed by God's consuming fire.

Feeling whole once again, I could perceive the voices of the missionaries as they returned from their day. I dashed downstairs to greet them and sent one of the female students, who would soon be entering a religious order, to the chapel to read from the text a few pages on religious life. Nina, however, returned empty-handed; the book was not there. (Later I discovered that one of the students had left it on purpose in case someone wanted to read it. He'd already picked it up. To this day, I believe that his leaving it there that morning was indeed a divine gesture of love.)

The last few days of the mission trip were filled with every experience of joy, and when I returned home, I discovered from a dear friend who happens to be very knowledgeable about Thérèse that the little saint read very few books in her lifetime, but she did read *The Imitation of Christ*. Perhaps my heavenly friend was with me in my suffering and she was a part of my learning to let go just a little more. I noticed in the weeks that followed a tremendous freedom from worry about my future and truly embraced the grace of the present moment.

Yielding and surrendering are perhaps the most central themes of my spiritual journey. Yet no matter how far along I am, I seem to get spiritually tongue-tied as I attempt to utter a mere yes. How important it is that I continue to pay attention to my struggles just long enough to hear the voice of the Master, beckoning me to himself. The rewards are profound.　　—R.H.

ஃ *St. Thérèse of Lisieux* ஃ

For me, prayer is an uplifting of the heart, a glance towards heaven, a cry of gratitude and of love in times of sorrow as well as joy. It is something noble, something supernatural, which expands the soul and unites it to God. —St. Thérèse, *Story of a Soul*

Thérèse Martin was born in France in 1873 to an extremely religious family, whose core values were confidence in God and total abandonment to his will. She was greatly influenced by the love of her beloved father, an experience that opened the way for a unique trust in her heavenly Father. By the time she was two and a half, Thérèse knew she wanted to be a nun, and at age nine she was convinced that she was born for glory and would in fact become a great saint. But her journey to sainthood involved tremendous loss and intense spiritual desolation, beginning with the death of her mother when Thérèse was only four, and then the loss of two of her sisters, who were like adopted mothers to Thérèse, to the monastery at Carmel. After her own entrance into the same cloister at the tender age of fifteen, Thérèse's sanctity grew as she struggled to embrace the hardships of life there: the austere environment at Carmel, harsh treatment by the nuns, her adored father's mental breakdown, his entrance into a hospital when Thérèse could do nothing about it, and finally her own grueling death from tuberculosis at age twenty-four. Thérèse described herself as "a little grain of sand in the desert that I chose."

Despite her brief life, Thérèse continues to captivate the hearts of thousands through her writings, created during her final years under obedience to the mother superior. Published exactly one year after her death, her autobiography became the spiritual classic Story of a Soul. *Within the text is an explanation of her "Little Way," the path of confidence and love that she saw as the way to heaven, unheard of at a time when much theology taught that heaven could be earned by just a few. Thérèse's spirituality embodied simply doing ordinary things with extraordinary love and trusting with total abandonment in God's mercy.*

After her canonization in 1925, Thérèse became one of the most beloved saints of all time, and in 1997 she was declared a Doctor of the Catholic Church by Pope John Paul II. Her spirituality, although deep and written about in flowery language, makes the journey so accessible, almost simple. According to Bishop Patrick Ahern, "The Little Way finds joy in the present moment, in being pleased to be the person you are, whoever you are. It is a school of self-acceptance, which goes beyond accepting who you are to wanting to be who you are. It is a way of coming to terms with life not as it might be but as it is."

I Was a Child, So Close to You

I cannot forget how the past is just behind us. . . .
When each thing is newly returned,
it is more difficult to turn away,
from the water's glistening sweep,
to let the least hour drift out of reach,
without wading in this river.
We each carry a child close against us,
And thigh deep in the gliding darkness,
this is another way to know,
the current pulls hard,
against our holding on.

—Julia B. Levine, "Walking Beside the American River,"
in *Practicing for Heaven*

LHD A recent morning found me deep in contemplation of Joyce Rupp's book *Cosmic Dance*. I gazed upon the lovely pastel illustrations that graced the book, painted so beautifully by Mary Southard, which is the story of our oneness with the earth, the universe, and God. I was preparing to do some writing to secure a contract, a project that had almost consumed me for days. I was stressed, and thin vapors of sadness curled around my heart. I felt lonely, yet, paradoxically, underneath the sadness lay joy: the joy of being willing to feel everything. I was willing to embrace the discomfort of the present moment and feel it all. Perhaps that is what being fully alive has always meant to me.

With the speed of light, a story emerged from the well of memory, presented to me in whole. I watched it, as one would a movie.

July 1956 . . . It was a summer's morning and a thin, sun-brown little girl of six, dressed in orange polka-dotted shorts, ran out of the old farmhouse she lived in, banging the sprung screen door behind her. The sun had barely reached the top of the trees.

Joyfully she dashed to her special place, a large, branching sycamore tree with a rope swing attached. But she didn't sit on the swing. She threw herself with sweet abandon into the lush clover beneath the tree. Nowhere in the whole yard did it grow as thick and soft as it did here. She lay on her back and gazed up through the sheltering branches of her tree to the washed blue sky above.

If she could have painted the scene, she would have shown cords of gold and silver that tied her both earthward and to the sky. She was enveloped in a great life force that she could only sense, a God not quite like church, a sheltering breast. She felt held and rocked and loved. A sense of coming from somewhere else, a sweet longing for another home filled her. Yet all was well, she wasn't lost, everything was tied together with those golden cords. Everything felt so close, almost touching distance. But she didn't think thoughts, she only felt. Sweet place, sweet love. All one, all safe. All Love.

That little girl was me.

After I wrote down this memory, I felt a bittersweet affection for that little girl, so fragile, innocent, and vulnerable — still newly arrived from some mysterious beginnings. I said with Kathleen Norris, "I once knew a little girl who lived in extraordinary closeness to the divine, as many children do." I experienced a deep nostalgia for that which I had lost, yet I was warmed, enlightened, and strengthened by this dear memory. I felt at once closer to God, my source. I recognized the invitation of God to welcome the child within me.

It reminded me of Jesus in Scripture and his love of little children: "He took a child and put him by his side and said to them, 'Whoever receives this child in my name receives me, and whoever receive me receives him who sent me; for he who is least among you all is the one who is great'" (Luke 9:47–48 NRSV).

And I realized then that my journey of prayer had in a way been a trip back, back to the place where this little girl rejoiced in wholeness and closeness to a sheltering breast that was God to her. These memories hold the key to nothing less than who I really am, a self lost to masks, facades, and cultural pressures.

The author Parker Palmer recently wrote that we are born with special gifts and abilities, and then we spend the first half of our lives turning our backs on them. When I read this commentary, I was thunderstruck. How true in my life! I thought with sadness.

And now in the second half of my life I feel as though I am answering a call by writing about ways to rediscover the fullness of the individuals that we are. We are souls created with infinite care, not one like another. And I hope that many of us will discover the child within us, this "least one," who is a key to what is great within us.

We are still the children we carry against us, thigh deep in the gliding darkness.   —L.H.D.

❧ *A Prayerful Life Review* ❧

Praying with graced history relies heavily on our faith memory (anamnesis) — a mystery in itself.
                                    —John English, S.J., *Spiritual Freedom*

I will present one method of mining memories that I feel is very useful in meditating upon one's personal history. In the beginning of an Ignatian retreat or walk with a spiritual director, the person being directed is invited to review and journal about his or her life in five- or ten-year segments. If you decide to do this, it may be helpful to look at your birth to age ten years in one-year increments, as these years are intensely formative. This review involves thinking and writing about the various stages in your life and looking at what was happening at these times. Questions include: Were you a healthy child? What state was your family in? Was it impacted by serious problems or deaths? Who were your good friends? What children were being born into your family? What were church and school like for you? What were your images of God and who taught them to you? These questions extend as marriage, work, and family years are explored, and the review continues to include your present circumstances and challenges.

As the review goes on, under the guidance of the director, you begin to discover the ways that God has been with you all along! Times of desolation are opened up and often show themselves to have been filled with God's mercy. Embrace times of consolation with gratitude. Examine with compassion the times you turned away from God and your true self and lost your way.

You may take this journey of memory on retreats, in spiritual direction or therapy, with a group of friends, or in private prayer, seeking help when you need it. I think that the spontaneous childhood memory that seemed to come effortlessly to me was actually excavated by much prayer and inner work.

Childhood memories hold many clues to who we are and why we act as we do. We may even find a roadmap to wholeness, to who we really are. In Behold Your Life, *Macrina Wiederkehr says simply, "God created me to be a blessing." In a life review, all the distanced parts of ourselves are embraced. We discover the many ways that God has always been with us bringing our blessed lives into full being, holding us with golden cords, calling us home to be blessings to ourselves and others.*

You Fulfill
My Deepest Desire

The spontaneous desires of our hearts are valuable clues to the will
of God for us.   —Wilkie Au, S.J., *By Way of the Heart*

Is not my house firm before God? He has made an eternal covenant
with me, set forth in detail and secured. Will he not bring to fruition
all my salvation and my every desire?   —2 Samuel 23:5 NAB

RH The first time I held Paula D'Arcy's book *Gift of the
Red Bird* I was startled by an odd sensation that felt
shamefully familiar and extremely uncomfortable: envy! Seated
at my friend Ellen's kitchen table, I'd opened Paula's book somewhere in the middle and truly just peeked in. In that one little
sneak preview I could tell that it seemed to contain all the
elements of the book I'd always dreamed of writing: journal
records, painful losses, and a life story. My soul resonated with
Paula's title because my own spiritual journey had contained a
string of connected events concerning birds. Why couldn't this
be *my* book?

How dare I, an adult woman, succumb to such a childish
emotion?! Book in hand, I was momentarily transported forty
years back to Mrs. Tilly's second-grade classroom. There, seated
among my peers, I had been an enthralled seven-year-old ob-
serving Shawn Collins show-and-tell the class about her new
Nifty binder. I didn't just want the binder. I wanted to *be* Shawn

64

confidently displaying *my* oratory skills as if I were demonstrating a product on a television commercial. Now, placing Paula's book back on the table where it waited to be wrapped for our friend as a get-well gift, I considered the thought that I wasn't ready to read it.

I had an appointment for spiritual direction the following week. In the midst of our session, Fr. Hampton caught me off guard with a very straightforward, yet provocative question: "Robin, what is your core desire?" I wasn't sure what he meant, but the word "desire" resonated with my yearning to write. As I spoke with him of my longing, I happened to glance at his overcrowded bookshelf, and there it was. *My* book! The one with the pretty red bird on the cover, written by a stranger who beat me to the punch. I grabbed the book off the shelf and held it in front of my heart as if I were guarding it.

"You see this book?" I asked rhetorically. "It was supposed to be *my* book!"

He looked at me lovingly and patiently, but a bit confused. Undaunted by my useless whining, he removed Paula's book from my hands, replaced it on the shelf, leaned in, looked squarely at me and spoke firmly: "Robin, if you want to write, then deepen your prayer life." I noted right then that he did *not* say: "Then go register at the local university for a class on creative writing." Fr. Hampton's words began to transform the passionate envy I felt, pointing to a new direction that would help actualize my deeply held desire. When I left his office, I felt freed and excited about what "deepening my prayer life" might mean.

I had already been experiencing the benefits of daily prayer, mostly through feelings of connectedness and joy. God had graced my life with amazing synchronicity and a great thirst for Scripture, so, the next morning, I settled into my regular prayer routine. As I sat in my prayer chair, it suddenly dawned on me that my relationship with God was becoming more familiar and comfortable, like an elderly couple sitting in side by side re- cliners. I welcomed this settled-in feeling. I felt secure, trusting that God would certainly lead me into a deepening experience with him.

On my morning walk that day, I prayed about my writing. It was as if God were saying, "Let me write your book for you. Just let it go." I mused on my friendly relationship with my Creator, so different from the God of my early years. Strolling along my familiar path beside the Vermilion River, I heard a declaration from deep inside: *"The God of my childhood was masculine. He was aloof, judgmental, and arrogant."* Joyfully, I felt in my heart I had just been given the first line of my book, and I thought that the theme of the book could be my experience of growing with God and healing my images of him. I felt exhilarated, yet detached from whether or not the writing would ever occur.

That same afternoon a friend unexpectedly offered me her copy of *Gift of the Red Bird.* I knew it was time to read it. As soon as I got home, I climbed the stairs to my bedroom and plopped in my special chair expectantly. Glancing at the clock, I was excited to see that I had a full hour to read before the kids got home from school. Reverently opening the book to chapter one, I read with astonishment, "The God of my child- hood was masculine. He was stern, judgmental, remote, and all-controlling." I was stunned, yet lifted into an experience of connection with God and with a total stranger, a new friend, a soul mate. I was captivated by the amazing coincidence and could hardly wait to embrace her words.

My heart raced as I devoured Paula's stunning narrative, raw with emotion, recounting how she came to terms with the loss of her husband and little daughter killed in a car accident by a drunk driver. I was even more mesmerized by her remarkable surrender throughout her story, and most especially in the delivery room as she gave birth to the child she was carrying at the time of the accident. God was speaking to me at the climax of her story: "Robin, I want you to want *me* more than you want *anything!*" I wanted to surrender as she had. I yearned to experience in my own life the universal story of death and resurrection, indeed the Paschal mystery, just as it was lived out through hers. Over the next several days, every chapter I read opened a new space in my soul where I could yield to trust, hope, wonder, and new insight. In her book, Paula showed me new pathways for my deepening journey.

By summer, I was on retreat with Paula and ready to embrace the new territory that beckoned me in her writing. Sitting in the chapel at the retreat center, I could feel the immense love generated by a woman of such small stature who had endured such enormous losses. Her piercing brown eyes revealed a wisdom so pure and deep. In spite of the fact that she had lost *everything,* she now seemed to have so very much — an open heart, a willing spirit, an awakened soul. Standing before me in her black linen jumper was a modern-day mystic with whom I could relate. She didn't live removed in a convent or cloister, but knew, as I did, the realities of marriage and the pains of child rearing. In an act certainly beyond the realities of my familiar culture, she had astonishingly forgiven the drunk driver responsible for the accident that took away her family. Hers was a voice of power, truth, and hope. I wanted such a courageous heart.

I attended several of her retreats, read her books, and became her friend. During a recent period in my life involving the gripping fear of a difficult transition, Paula happened to be staying at my home. As we visited over tea at my kitchen island, she listened to my pain and spoke with candor, reminding me of a familiar reality: "When we're living out of the false self, there's drama, suffering, and pain. The true self is an inward spring where there's strength and peace."

I could feel my heart settling down in her tender care and could access the strength she spoke of. My soul sister encouraged me to continue to awaken and frankly warned that if I didn't, I'd keep getting lost in drama. Then she spoke a bold truth, the power of which carved greater depths into my novice spirit. Her words sounded prophetic: "An unawakened spirit is not available in life or death. It's why you can waste a lifetime. Then the life doesn't produce anything."

Those words sunk into my deepest self. . . . *An unawakened spirit is not available in life or death.* The thought that I could not only waste a lifetime *now,* but also even after my passing, gave way to strength, hope, and a fierce commitment to moving beyond being a victim. I pondered, How can I awaken so that my life might mean something? What does it mean to my soul to be available in death? What is it that I want my life to produce?

Those questions have become core to my journey, and I have revisited them time and again, finding the answers hidden most often in the little things that make me happy, like spending precious time with my grandchildren and knowing my presence in their lives matters, or sitting across from a directee in a spiritual direction session sharing joyfully in a personal triumph. Sometimes, like this morning, my life means something simply because of a heart-to-heart conversation with my daughter-in-law. *This I know....* It's my love I want to leave behind, the fire in my heart for God and for the priceless people he so carefully places on my path. My hope is that my presence in others' lives will bring them one step closer to the Mystery of Love in their own lives long after I am gone.

The writing of this book has certainly been a part of that awakening. Mostly, my writing has helped me to relive and to embrace much more deeply the daily awakenings that have transpired over my journey. I don't ever remember feeling so excited and alive! Sometimes on my best days it *has* felt like God has inspired my writing, fulfilling the promise he made to me on my morning walk so long ago. I am left with the thought that our deepest desires lead us to the ways God wants to work through us. Perhaps Fr. Hampton's question "What is your core desire?" was meant to simply awaken me to one of those ways so that I, like Hildegard of Bingen, could become a feather on the breath of God. I thank you, God, for bringing to fruition even this desire.

—R.H.

⁓ε *What Is a Spiritual Director?* ℥⁓

A spiritual director is facilitator of the spiritual journey who is, foremost, someone grounded in prayer and in a deep desire to grow in intimacy with God. He or she assists another, the directee, to advance on that path. The director is not a therapist or a counselor, but is a spiritual companion. The focus in this ministry is not on problems, but on prayer; not on the grumble of life, but on growth. Through deep, contemplative listening, the spiritual director assists the directee in prayerfully discerning the movements of the Holy Spirit, thus helping him or her to listen, respond, and grow.

How does one know if he or she is ready to receive spiritual direction? Basically, it is a calling. Inherent in the calling is a strong commitment to regular prayer (if you're not praying, there's nothing to talk about). Spiritual direction also requires a desire to grow, as well as a willingness to intimately share the journey with another. A person ready for spiritual direction longs to develop his or her own relationship with God, but is also looking for assistance to go deeper, and to be held accountable to stay committed to the journey. The first step, then, is to pray, asking God: "Is spiritual direction something you are calling me to explore?"

The following are hints to help you find a qualified spiritual director:

- *Ask God in prayer to reveal to you a person who you might feel safe with as you risk sharing your faith journey.*

- *Sometimes a priest or minister can offer spiritual direction or at least assist with referrals. (Just because one is a member of the clergy or a religious order does not mean that he or she would qualify as a good director. Many who are involved in full-time ministry struggle to find the time to offer regular spiritual direction, or they may lack ministerial experience or formal training.)*

- *Professional organizations such as Spiritual Directors International maintain lists of qualified spiritual directors. They can be contacted online at www.sdiworld.org or by phone (425-455-1565); they can make suggestions for referrals in your area.*

- *Consider contacting retreat centers, monasteries, or communities of religious orders in your area.*

- *As in seeking other professional services, word of mouth is often the best method.*

- *If you cannot find a certified spiritual director, consider seeking the support of a spiritual friend, one who doesn't give advice or offer judgments and has a prayerful, reflective, contemplative spirit.*

Finally, spiritual direction is a beautiful ministry that is gaining popularity in spiritual circles. Lyn and I are blessed by our experiences both personally as directees and professionally as spiritual directors, and we pray that you can find a director if it is indeed a desire of your heart.

Your Beautiful World Fills Me

Everything that is in the heavens, on the earth, and under the earth, is penetrated with connectedness, is penetrated with relatedness.

—Hildegard of Bingen

I am the vine, you are the branches. He who abides in me, and I in him, he it is that bears much fruit, for apart from me you can do nothing.

—John 15:5 NRSV

LHD It was six o'clock on a summer's morning as I stepped along the highway carefully, looking for cars approaching in the fog. I walked to exercise, to pray, and to think.

If I could have cut and sewn the dewy grass I walked upon, I would have fashioned a sparkly blouse, the kind worn at holiday parties. As I looked about, I saw the changes that recent rains had brought. The trees along the way were a heavy canopy of green. In the ditch, the tall, wiry grass was bent into loops, like hundreds of croquet wickets thrust willy nilly into the earth. Nearby, wild sunflowers waved golden and happy in the filtered light. I rejoiced in the abundance of summer.

I had been reading the life of Hildegard of Bingen in the historical novel *Scarlet Music*. A passionate reader, I often encountered books I could hardly put down, and this was

one. The lady from medieval times had captured my imagination, and she even appeared in my prayers. The depth of
her creativity stunned me; she was a prolific writer, visionary,
artist, herbalist, composer of music, church activist, and more.
She struggled with prejudices against the spiritual thoughts of
women within herself and her church in order to speak in her
authentic voice.

As I walked on, it occurred to me that the natural scene
I now beheld was little different from Hildegard's world eight
hundred years ago. She loved the earth and its blooming, "the
exquisite greening of trees and flowers." Living in a rich area of
the Rhine Valley she delighted in the changing of the seasons
and the abundance of the earth. The Rhine Valley had a wealth
of vineyards, and so the biblical images of the vine and its
fruit were never far from Hildegard's mind. Jesus himself used
these images as symbols of our connectedness to him, saying,
"Abide in me as I abide in you. Just as the branch cannot bear
fruit by itself unless it abides in the vine, neither can you unless
you abide in me" (John 15:4 NRSV).

As Hildegard lived, worked, and prayed in her fertile valley,
she coined a word to describe this world of greenness and the
unity of enlivening spirit that she observed in all life: *veriditas*.
Her newly minted term combined two Latin words, *viriditas*,
meaning "greenness," and *veritas*, meaning "truth." Green-
truth. I paused my walking for a moment as I remembered that
for Hildegard, Spirit's breath constantly animated the world.
She saw no separation between the natural world and God,
between humans and their natural environment. Her visions
were of a rich, organic whole, with God breathing life into all. In
Jesus, Hildegard finds "Greenness Incarnate." Jesus enlivens

that part of us that is the life force of our bodies, our souls, the sparkling fire of creation within us.

I continued walking and rounded a curve, noticing a pasture ahead on my left. The cattle there, still partly obscured by mist, were blurry rectangles of cream and brown. As I walked nearer, a calf raised his vulnerable little head and looked at me, his magnolia-leaf ears springing up in alertness. Wide marble eyes regarded me seriously. Perhaps I looked dangerous. I smiled at him, feeling a tender connection within me. He was a part of the life of creation; "God burning everywhere." Ah, tender fire, you fill me.

Hildegard had a cosmic vision of the God of creation: "I the supreme and fiery force who has kindled all sparks of life and breathe forth none of death and I judge them as they are. . . . I, the fiery life of the divine substance, blaze in the beauty of the fields, shine in the waters, and burn in the sun, moon, and stars. And as the all-sustaining invisible force of the aerial wind, I bring all things to life."

These words filled me with their beauty and excitement — their life-force. I sat upon a bench in a little park to think. A car stopped, and a man looked out of his rolled-down window. For a moment, I was wary. There had been a serial killer in the area, and my consciousness was saturated with fear. Then I looked closely at his concerned eyes and I relaxed. I felt in my spirit that he was not dangerous. "You all right, m'am?" he asked.

I replied, "Yes, I'm fine. Just resting during my walk."

He was young and I saw that he had a baby chair in his backseat. I probably reminded him of his mother, or perhaps he was an off-duty police officer. At any rate, I felt somehow reconnected. How kind it was of him to check on me! He drove on.

I pondered a little more about how all our fears separate us, from the earth and from each other. I pulled a small notebook from my pocket and wrote, "You are the vine; we are the branches. Show us, God, how to abide in you, and to honor your fantastic green life in all the earth: in nature, animals, and people. Let me breathe the fiery breath of your life. Let me dance with joy, reverently and kindly upon this earth."

Writer Cindy Crosby says of her experience with the natural world, "There's a skin of the landscape I'm beginning to peel back, and I'm finding a map of sorts in the world around me, a landscape of prayer; creation cannot help but praise the creator. Symbols of the landscape beckon me further up and deeper in."

"Further up," I thought. "Deeper in... and further down. Connect me, O God, to you in this sweet earth, to *veriditas*."

It had been a good walk indeed. I had made a four-mile circle that had brought me back to my starting place. It was time to stop, because the dampness had penetrated the seams of my tennis shoes and my socks were wet. My soul was watered too, and I felt more connected, not so alone. The sun had at last burned through the tulle curtain of mist and shone upon my face.

I reflected that as a writer I was much alone and sometimes lonely, but perhaps loneliness was not my main problem. The problem was the original sin of alienation that I shared with so many: we believed we were separated from God within us, from one another, and from the earth. A cursory glance at our world revealed the disastrous effects of our schisms. "Connect us back, God," I prayed, "or at the very least, let us be *willing* to live as one."

My dogs, Taffy and Charlie, dashed up the drive to meet me, tongues and tails wagging as bright sunshine warmed the top of my head. Vibrant green was everywhere. I was home.

—L.H.D.

❧ A Poem Prayer, Veriditas ❧

There is a quality of light today,
So green, just born of Eden.
It touches my face and whispers,
"Come away and be with me."
*   Dare I put the burdens down,*
The busyness and questing for more?
The more that is never enough,
And the being good,
That is never good enough.
*   I follow the light, and I become,*
A part of it.
Veriditas!
Sweet creation . . . where everything I need
Is already present.
Within and around me.
Wrapping me in a soft quilt of breathing-life,
Of Love in all Its forms.

There is a quality of light today,
Fire of creation, warming my breath.
You are well, dear one, it says.
As you are now.
And you are one with Me, Voice whispers,
without strife or suffering,
Without separation.
For how could I, your God, reject,
A part of my own great heart?

Within You
Is My True Home

"Home" is a rich symbol with many layers of meaning. It is a paradigm, an exemplary symbol of harmony and wholeness. "Home" gives us our place in the world. It roots us in the earth.... We go back home in order to find our truest self.
— Thomas Merton, as quoted in *Journeys into Emptiness*

RH Being attached to a home may seem *unspiritual* to some, but most women know better. Our domain is sacred. It provides the setting for the very best of our lives — nesting, nurturing, homemaking, childrearing — all very divine purposes indeed.

In the summer of 1979, with one toddler and a baby on the way, my husband and I moved our little family into the cutest house in the whole of Lafayette, Louisiana! Perched on a corner, it looked like a little French cottage. Pretty ruffled curtained windows were adorned with red geraniums growing profusely below in window boxes. The limestone circular front driveway, like outstretched arms, offered a warm, welcoming presence. Covered in ivy, the house appeared to be tucked in the enchanted forest of a fairy tale. It truly exuded warmth and hospitality. Moreover, the home also reflected our family persona in that it looked good on the outside but was sometimes very messy on the inside.

Being an avid gardener, I could hardly wait until our first spring. By then the baby was several months old, and I could get out into the yard to build my first garden. The very day I ordered a load of dirt, my husband came home from work with the proclamation, "Cancel the dirt! There's a bridge coming through our house!" He had encountered someone that day who had informed him of a city plan for a bridge that would indeed cut right through our property. The left-handed blessing of that announcement was that, as much as I loved my home, I learned from the beginning not to hold on too tightly.

As with many urban projects, however, the plan for the bridge didn't exactly get off the ground in a timely fashion. Nineteen years later, I was still digging in those flower beds and pasting the walls with wallpaper. We had raised four children, enjoyed countless birthday parties, and bandaged many knees. The house had staged lemonade stands, slumber parties, and the annual Christmas photo taken of the kids on the stairway, a picture that always seemed to capture their eager anticipation of what Santa might have placed under the tree. We had loved and buried dogs, cats, fish, and hamsters there. Sadly, even our marriage was buried there. Yet the home had endeared itself to all of us, and in every way for us it was a sacred dwelling.

After years of neighborhood petitions and failed political schemes, the city was finally on track with its plans for the Camellia Boulevard Bridge that would dislocate eighty families. Information meetings began in the church hall across the street from my home. Those gatherings were tense and full of emotion, since homesteads are sacred to everyone. Nevertheless, the bridge was imminent.

I began to pray earnestly that God would find our next home and that the city would treat us fairly. I really didn't want to get caught up in all the drama. One of my greatest concerns was that I still had two teenagers at home and I knew this move would be a difficult one for them.

In the weeks following the first town meeting, I began noticing sparrows everywhere, especially around my property. A mother sparrow had built a nest in the carport, and every time I drove in I was greeted by the swarming of little brown birds welcoming me home. One morning in prayer, I turned to Psalm 84 and was lifted immediately into consolation....

> How lovely your dwelling, O Lord of Hosts!
> My soul yearns and pines for the courts of the Lord.
> My heart and flesh cry out for the living God.
> As the sparrow finds a home and the swallow a nest to
>   settle her young,
> My home is by your altars....
> Happy are those who dwell in your house!
> They never cease to praise you. (Ps. 84:2–5)

As a sparrow finds a home.... God had touched me with a faithful promise, and from that day forward I seemed to know that I, too, would find a home to settle my young. God also seemed to be reminding me that my true home is in his very heart.

The following summer, with two kids off to college, I moved with my other two children, Emily and Michael, into another wonderful little nest to set up a new household, on Memory Lane, no less! (I liked to refer to it as *New* Memory Lane!) The transition was somewhat difficult for the kids, but over time they settled in.

Still another year went by, and an official from the city called to inform me that our beloved former home would be torn down the next day. I was almost relieved, since it had been difficult to pass by and see it so untended. The ivy had taken over like a cancer and was growing through the windows. Doors and windows had been removed. Of course the yard was terribly overgrown. That day, I gathered the kids so we could bid farewell, and our grieving began all over again.

Our wake was bittersweet. As a family, we walked through each room and spontaneously began telling stories. Good memories were shared with lots of giggles....

"Do you remember the day Michael emptied out his bedroom through that window?" When Michael was about two, he got the wild idea to throw every item he could put his hands on out of his second-story window. Blankets had hung down the side of the house like a fire escape. Game-board pieces, teddy bears, and toys were spread throughout the garden. It was really kind of funny, although it's funnier now than it was then. After all, he could've thrown himself out.

Slapping his knee, Ryan acted like an impish eight-year-old again, as he burst out laughing at the dents in Megan's bedroom door, the one he tried to kick in the day she had locked him out as they had fought over the remote control.

They remembered with fondness the hide-and-seek games, the mudhole the boys built as a swimming pit in the back yard, and the hilarious episodes that we never got around to sending into *America's Funniest Home Videos*. All these seemingly insignificant events, when pasted together, indeed make a family.

As I returned for the last time to the kitchen, the heart and soul of any home, I noticed the mustard-colored wallpaper with the little rust flowers still pasted to the ceiling. Everything else had been stripped. The kitchen cabinets with the chicken wire inserts, some of the Mexican tile from the counter tops, the tall picture window, and the wooden beams from the ceiling were all gone. I felt like I was standing in the middle of a burial mound. And then my eye caught a balled-up burlap object lying on the floor. I reached down to open it up and was confused for a moment as I searched my memory for clues as to what this was.

Then it dawned on me that it was a banner made for us many years before by friends. We were pregnant with Emily, our third child, at the time. On the banner was a green grapevine with five purple grapes and a saying: "Our family . . . growing towards new life!" I realized that the banner had been stuffed on top of one of the kitchen cabinets and had fallen during their removal. But what a timely message now, that day, a reminder of the promise of new life. I was amazed by the synchronicity, in which a scarred and battered kitchen had become, for me, an altar of God's grace. I thanked God again that he had cared for me and my little family just as he promises to take care of the sparrows.

Months later, I received the most special and thoughtful gift of my life. My friend Chuck had gone to the property the day the house had been torn down. He had collected remnants from the piles of debris and had fashioned them into a little grotto for my garden. The flowered Mexican tile from my kitchen adorned the inside. Pieces of the wooden fence and a rose-colored fragment of my bedroom window frame decorated the outside. Chuck had even placed on it a cross, formed from an iron grate that had served as an attic vent. I wept with gratitude for the keepsake and for the love that had gone into its creation.

The kids are all gone now. In fact, I lived on Memory Lane for only a few years and now reside with my second husband in a lovely home, one I am much less attached to, thank God. But new memories are created daily through our own lives as well as through our six kids, three of *their* beloved spouses, eight grandchildren, and the many friends that we now share.

The grotto stands in my garden today as a shelter for St. Francis and a reminder that my home is indeed by God's altars, no matter where that might be.   —R.H.

❧ *Lectio Divina* ❧

In Everything Belongs, *Richard Rohr states, "In our culture, we suffer from, among other things, a glut of words, a glut of experiences, and yes, a glut of tapes, books, and ideas. We can't absorb it all. . . . We desperately need some disciplines to help us know how to see and what is worth seeing, and what we don't need to see." I believe that* lectio divina *is one such discipline.*

Lectio divina, *literally "divine reading," is a form of prayer I use almost daily. Resurrected from the Desert Fathers, it has been written about frequently in recent years. I learned to practice* lectio *with the help of several Benedictine sisters, as this form of prayer is a cherished part of their monastic tradition. It is far from a Scripture study, for it calls forth a response from the heart, not the head. It is not about understanding, but about* living *the Word.*

I like to think of lectio *as sitting in the chamber of your heart waiting for the divine gift of God's Word. You know it has arrived when the heart stirs.*

Here's how lectio divina *works:*

First, read a chosen passage from Scripture, slowly and re-flectively. Read with a receptive heart, one that is open and willing to be changed, with a longing to be touched by God through his Word. I usually select the daily Scripture readings from the Catholic liturgical year, but you could pray a psalm every day, journey through the Gospels one chapter at a time, or simply open the Bible and randomly choose a passage.

Second, read the same passage a second time and then stop when your heart has been moved, to meditate on the word or phrase that has stirred you. Consider questions such as "How do these words touch my life today?" and "God, what are you asking of me, affirming in me, or challenging me to change?"

Third, pray in response to the stirring, as if to answer an invitation. In prayer, the listening and speaking begin. Engage your heart in order to hear those answers and respond some-how, perhaps in words, in images, or even in tears. Afterward you may be left with a phrase that can be used throughout that day as a prayer mantra: "The Lord is my shepherd"; "Lord, help my unbelief"; "A clean heart create for me"; "Be still and know that I am God."

Finally, enter contemplation, letting go of all of the words and images, resting in God for a while. It's like enjoying the quiet companionship of a good friend. I use my breath and often a mantra to help me get to that quiet, restful state, and when I can, I try to stay there for twenty minutes or so.

After practicing lectio *for years, I now begin with contem-plation because it seems to prepare my heart for the reading; I end with journaling. It's a wonderful way to begin the day!*

Finally, Macrina Wiederkehr, herself a Benedictine, offers timeless advice for practicing lectio divina *in her spiritual classic,* A Tree Full of Angels: *"Always read the Scriptures with a heart ready to repent." With conversion of heart, mind, and will as an ongoing goal of prayer, one word, image, or phrase can be enough to provide the change of a lifetime.*

I Trust You
Down a Twisting Path

And those who know your name put their trust in you, for you, O Lord, have not forsaken those who seek you.

—Psalm 9:10 NRSV

To walk the sacred path is to discover our inner sacred space, that core of being that is waiting to have life breathed back into it.

—Lauren Artress, *Walking a Sacred Path*

LHD The labyrinth behind Hospice of Acadiana in Lafayette sat near one of the busiest intersections of the city. I had been told about it by my friend Joan, who lost her husband three years ago. She was instrumental in the creation of a small prayer garden containing this labyrinth, which was modeled on the one at Chartres Cathedral in France. Its presence at the hospice center allowed those in grief or transition to use the meditative practice of walking the labyrinth, but it was also sought out by people like me, who used it regularly for prayer.

One morning, I parked my car near the Albertson's grocery store and walked easily to the labyrinth, painted in purple and cream directly on the cement of the parking lot nearby. As I studied it, a lady came out of the hospice building and smiled at me. "Here to walk the labyrinth?" she said. "Do you know anything about it?"

"Well, I have been doing some reading," I replied. "But I would be grateful for any information."

"It's really very simple. One way in and one way out. Some people like to walk the lunations around the outside to get centered. Just relax and enjoy it." She handed me a brochure and said goodbye.

I began to walk the outside circle, stepping on each lunation, or half-circle, that adorned the outside edge of the labyrinth. This forced me to walk slowly, like taking baby steps in the "Mother, may I?" game.

I breathed, in out, in out. My attention was centered on my feet. Time slowed. The noise of those arriving at Albertson's or whizzing by on Johnston Street receded. I was alone.

Having finished the outside circle of the labyrinth, I arrived at its entrance and stopped. I had done some reading about this ancient meditation, and so I knew that one thing to do when entering was to focus on an intention, a desire of the heart. I did this, saying simply, "Teach me what I need to know." I said this several times, quietly and slowly. I entered. The path was a series of loops; they did not confuse or trick but merely guided, forcing me to pay attention and to be fully present in each moment. As Eckhart Tolle states in *The Power of Now*, "Taking responsibility for this moment means not to oppose internally the suchness of Now, not to argue with what is. It means to be in alignment with life. . . . Now is the only place that life can be found."

As I walked I found it was necessary to concentrate, but in a relaxed way. I noticed that it was impossible for me to predict where the path would lead. Since my mind couldn't decipher the pattern, my body let go. The cream color of the path was pretty against its purple outline. I noticed the cracks that invited the grass to grow through, which reminded me that this practice was not about perfection. There was peace in having such a simple delineated task, free from competing claims upon my energies and attention. About halfway through the walk to the center, I felt the word "trust." I was surprised.

Continuing, I arrived at the center of the labyrinth, where a scalloped rose was painted in cream against purple. I stood, looking outward and turning about. The labyrinth seemed to vibrate around me. I felt a gentle, embracing energy coming from the enclosing circle. I heard internally, "You do not trust. I have brought you this far. Trust."

I left the center too soon, but then I was sorry. I wanted to jump back in, but not wanting to cheat, I continued out. "One way in, one way out." What the lady said was true. I had the urge to rush out because I wanted to think about walking to the center again while I could. I forced myself to slow down. Now drawn close to the center, now thrown far away, now close again. The center. "God, you are the center," I prayed. "Trust," God replied silently in my heart.

Suddenly, I was led out, and I stood outside the labyrinth and studied it. Hildegard of Bingen says that God is "the divine spiral, a circle, a wheel, a whole." Had I walked into a metaphor for God? For my journey into God?

The labyrinth has existed in simple forms since prehistoric times and is found in all cultures around the globe. The walking of the labyrinth gained prominence as a spiritual practice in the Middle Ages, during the time that Hildegard lived. Chartres Cathedral was built during this era and features the most famous labyrinth of them all. This eleven-circuit creation is centered with a rose in honor of the Blessed Virgin and is set into the floor of the famous church.

During that era the labyrinth was walked by believers either at the culmination of a pilgrimage to the Holy Land or in lieu of such a trip. It symbolizes the journey and a going forth, as well as arriving. Its circular shape is the mandala, symbolizing wholeness of the self.

The sound of Lafayette traffic filled my ears again. I went to the nearby grove of trees and sat on the concrete bench; I pulled Lauren Artress's book on the labyrinth out of my purse and I read, "The labyrinth introduces us to the idea of a wide and gracious path. It redefines the journey to God: from a vertical perspective that goes from earth up to heaven, to a horizontal perspective in which we are all walking the path together."

Artress says that over the centuries the vertical path has gotten mired down in perfectionism and elitism. On the labyrinth road we walk together, at once losing and finding our way. I understood that the labyrinth was telling me that a key to my path is to walk in trust.

I took out my journal. "Trust," I wrote. In what ways did I not trust? Answers came quickly.

My life and my work had been changing. I worried about my writing career. I worried about my husband and son. I worried about my property and my money and my aging parents. God called me to trust him and be contented with all the gifts of my life. My demons had been calling the beat to a different dance, a dance of relentless productivity, discontent, and fear.

A dance of the ego, for sure.

I created another journal entry: "Help me to trust, Lord, to take the baby steps around the edges. Lead me in this walk. Teach me not to be greedy for success, for more, more, more of everything. I want to rejoice in all you have given me and abide in your love. I put my worries in your hands. Give me a heart of service." I sat quietly with this prayer request for many minutes, repeating the word "trust" on each breath and feeling peace and happiness rise within me.

Then I rose and entered the labyrinth again, walking even slower. I breathed deeply in and out. Suddenly, I started to feel playful. I skipped, I hopped, I sang. I had slipped into the joyful trust of childhood. Now my prayer was one of praise: "God is good and my life is God's song!" I warbled. "Da,da,da,da,da, da, da, da." I didn't need any more words for my little composition. As I hopped from one foot to the other in the looping spirals, I knew something at the level of my heart. I might forget it on another day, but for this day I knew: prayers do get answered. —L.H.D.

God, I Need You More Than Ever

As a mother comforts her son, so I will comfort you.
—Isaiah 66:13a NAB

Surrender is being willing rather than willful. It is a readiness to trust that is based in love. It is relaxing and letting go. It is floating in the river that is God's love. —David G. Benner, *Surrender to Love*

RH Plopped on the timber edging of a rose bed at a nearby church one evening, I allowed myself to sink into the despair that days before had erupted in my spirit. Less than a year after our wedding, my new husband and I were embracing some of the challenges that often accompany a second, midlife marriage, namely, the kids. He was struggling with some of the choices mine were making. I was in a tailspin over the discomfort of his judgments. But the real issue was my fear of abandonment, my childhood wound that would flare when the conditions were right.

As I grew still, the tears flowed. I realized how scared I was and told God about it. Just expressing my fear felt good. I shared my heartache as well as my shameful human urge to try to control others' lives. I expressed how helpless I felt struggling to trust him with my life, my marriage, and the lives of my loved ones. Feeling the safety and comfort of the moment, I went deeper into the anguish of feeling alone and unloved and

I began to weep as I unloaded this burden that I seemed to have kept hidden even from myself. I was truly surprised by the depths of my pain. I seemed to hear him whisper, "Just let me love you," a statement that was to be the core of my journey over the next several months.

The next morning, while strolling to my neighborhood exercise class, I was suddenly comforted by a vision of Jesus standing before me, cupping my face in his hands. He seemed to be walking right there with me and had just stopped to offer this gesture of love. It was a fleeting, yet unforgettable image. He wasn't going to let me go one more day with that unloved, abandoned feeling that had consumed me the night before. In that instant, I wasn't alone anymore.

I went on to class, but my mind seemed to wander back to the powerful words I'd heard in the garden the previous evening. I silently uttered, "How can I let you love me?" He seemed to offer a very specific suggestion: go to the Jesuit Spirituality Center in the nearby town of Grand Coteau. It was as if Jesus were inviting me to come away with him for the weekend.

I recalled that I was giving a retreat there in a few weekends and needed a little prep time. Yet I know only too well that preparation is mostly about doing for myself what I ask retreatants to do: be still and bask in God's love. And what a place to do that! Magnificent oak trees, rocking chairs, and walking paths surround the retreat center. The silence and solitude of the environment are balm for any soul. Just being on the property and in the welcoming presence of the religious that live and work there is a loving experience. It felt right to spend the weekend on that holy ground.

When I got home from class, there was a message to call my former husband. I made the reservation at the center and then returned the call. To my shock and utter dismay, he informed me of a crisis involving our eighteen-year-old son, Michael, resulting from some poor choices he had made. Feeling victimized by my son's bad judgment, my heart was torn in two. Of course part of me wanted to run to comfort him, while another side wished I could turn him over my knee, something I would never do. More than anything I desired to coddle him like I did when he was a little boy, making up stories to soothe his pain. When I arrived in his presence, I was unprepared for the image before me of a young man who was totally withdrawn and dejected. Compassion flooded my heart. I cupped his face in my hands and reminded him of my love as well as the heartache of my disappointment. We cried together as we both shared our concerns. It was important to me to convey to him that no matter what, I would never abandon him.

The biggest hurdle came in bearing the truth to my husband, Easton, later on that morning. Although married briefly, whenever we had faced challenges, he tended to withdraw and I fell into old patterns of trying to fix. I wanted to make everything better, to somehow make the situation go away. I was frightened to bear the truth to Easton, not wanting to make my son look bad in his eyes. I needed his support and so did Michael.

In a grace-filled insight, I drew on an analogy of the replay of a championship tennis match we'd watched on television the night before in which a dehydrated Pete Sampras came back to win the U.S. Open. While we were watching the match, I'd asked Easton, a seasoned tennis player, how Sampras did that. His response had been quick: "He dug deeper into himself to find the strength to fight on." Sitting on our bed explaining the situation involving my son, I asked Easton to do what Pete had done and then dragged my heavy heart with me to Grand Coteau. I knew I would have to do the same.

GLANCING AROUND my sparsely furnished room in Grand Coteau, I felt comforted by the familiar surroundings and simplicity of the décor. Sitting on my single bed, I peered at the wooden crucifix hanging on the wall across from me. Jesus felt very present to me as I related to his pain of bearing the tensions for those he loved. I asked Jesus to be my spiritual director for the weekend and invited him to point me to appropriate Scripture, leading me to what I most needed to hear and experience. I'd brought with me not only my Bible, but also a few books on St. Thérèse of Lisieux. The retreat I was to give in several weeks was centered on her spirituality and I had not had time to read one rather complex text, *The Power of Confidence*. I inscribed these words in my journal as I entered prayer: "Only by your grace and my obedience am I here. . . . *God, I need you more than ever.*"

A response came quickly. One of the first Scripture passages I was led to was Isaiah 66:13, one of Thérèse's favorites. In fact, it was the very one that helped her to formulate the core of her spirituality, her "Little Way," as she called it. As I read the prophet's words, I shuddered with amazement and wept in reassurance that I was being held by an Almighty presence loving me beyond my limited imagination: "As a mother comforts her son, so I will comfort you." I felt like a participant in holy mystery, partaking as both giver and receiver of the divine embrace. I truly sensed being held in his arms and swaddled in his love, and I felt grateful that I had done the same for my hurting son only hours earlier.

That afternoon, I studied Thérèse's painful journey and began to compare elements of hers to my own. Agonizing trials had purified her desire to become a nun and helped to stabilize her vocation. I wondered about my own desires and questioned their purity. Was my need to stabilize my children's lives a selfish attempt to bring order to my own? Was I unwilling to bear their turmoil because I wanted a comfortable existence?

And then I read that Thérèse believed that God sent her trials so that she might desire *nothing*, not even what she believed to be the best for others or herself. I pondered the fact that I truly don't know what is best for myself or another. I felt helpless and vulnerable, yet strengthened and supported by her great faith and tender confidence in God. She lived certain of God's intervention and in fact saw human weakness as provoking it. She looked at suffering as not just useful but *necessary* in order to love.

I spent much of the weekend walking the grounds and crying, totally embracing my heartache. The trees, the quiet, the utter stillness absorbed the tears and eased my pain. Abandoning my perceived needs to God's loving care seemed to be my greatest struggle. Feeling like I was in a boat lost at sea, I could only pray that Jesus would get me to safe shores and to beautiful new lands. That weekend, he never let me be alone in my pain. He was in my boat all along. Every word, reflection, prayer, and image seemed to soothe my soul and provide solace for that desolate place in my life.

The climax of my weekend came with an image I received as I completed my reading about Thérèse that spoke of this exact juncture on my journey. Thérèse saw herself as a little child at the foot of a long staircase, looking up to her Father standing at the top of the steps. As she placed her foot on that first step, in his almighty love, God swooped down to draw her up to him. I became that child at the bottom of the stairwell, fearfully carrying the burdens that were still weighing me down. Placing my foot on the first step was simply an act of desire to let go. God did the rest. He did the surrendering for me. I have drawn on the grace of that momentous insight many times since. I cannot relinquish anything on my own. All I can do is desire to surrender, and God does the rest.

I would never suggest that my return home turned into happily ever after. The crises were there waiting for me. In fact, I quickly discovered that nobody had changed but me. Yet the strength and confidence I gained on those two brief days from the grace of God's loving care fortified me for the weeks ahead. Feeling freed somewhat from my need to control, I seemed to be filled with trust as I faced tough personal situations. I have realized in looking back on that time of struggle that my experiences of great consolation are the very essence of what sustain me on the journey, especially when the road seems most treacherous.

—R.H.

⚘ *Journaling as a Spiritual Practice* ⚘

We often refer in our essays to journal use, as both Lyn and I find it a helpful spiritual practice. (I even learned from her when I read her book Water from Stones *the importance of using a good pen.) I have journaled for many years and consider the practice an intimate record of the movements of the*

Spirit within my own heart, even referring to my journal as my best friend!

Perhaps this practice has been easier for us to embrace because we both love to write. However, this form of expression has little to do with style, correctness, or beauty of phrase. This is the soul expressing itself on paper and bringing the unseen to light. Journaling can help stop confused thinking, when fears and darkness circulate in our heads and we can't make sense of things. On the other hand, it is also good to record those precious, happy times of consolation in order to truly thank God for them and to come back to them during darker days. Mostly, it is a way to know what we really feel beneath our masks and social skills, a way to honor the authentic self and learn to know this self as loved and cared for by God.

Here are some simple ideas and guidelines from both of us for journaling:

- *Your journal is confidential. Keep it in a safe place where you can trust that others won't read it. You must be allowed to write in freedom and honesty.*

- *Don't worry about neatness, grammar, or form. Get your ideas and feelings down on paper.*

- *Start wherever you are: desolation, dryness, or joy. Write about the weather, your broken car, the way you are feeling, or whatever is happening in your life. The rule here is that there are no rules. This writing is just for you and God.*

- *Consider using it for gratitude. Nothing assists our spirits more when we are down than to write about even the little things that we have to be thankful for, a conversation with one of the kids, an image from nature, a day off, time with a friend, husband, etc. There are so many people, events, and blessings for which to be thankful. Writing it down seems to help us remember the important practice of gratitude, which always lifts our spirits.*

- *Choose a pretty journal that you like, perhaps one that is bound. Don't make do with someone's tossed aside notebook. Be sure your journal is big enough and doesn't make your writing feel cramped. Note if you prefer a lined journal or one without lines. Have a nice pen that writes well. Lyn likes to use thin colored markers to highlight or illustrate, or paste pictures from magazines that move her heart.*

- *Write little poems that no one but you will read. Be silly. Be angry. Write prayers, ask questions, draw pictures. Write about a Scripture or sermon that has struck you and how it might affect your everyday life. Write about past events that have hurt you or lifted you up. Journal about those close to you and the state of your relationships. Look at your own behavior. Repeating yourself is fine; just tell the truth.*

- *Write first thing in the morning if possible, and just after prayer. In* The Artist's Way, *Julia Cameron calls this, "Cleaning the window." Sometimes it can make your day much better as negative feelings get cleared away.*

Soon you may discover that you want to take your journal everywhere to record your experiences. There are many good books available about this practice, and also books that provide readings and then corresponding journaling questions. We like all these ways of journaling. Find the ways that enliven and inform your heart and deepen your relationship with God and with yourself.

God, Please Forgive Me

Why do you see the speck that is in your brother's eye, but do not notice the log that is in your own eye?　　　—Luke 6:41 NRSV

The way of prayer brings us face to face with the shame and indignity of the false self that seeks to live for itself alone.
　　　—Thomas Merton as quoted in *Journeys into Emptiness*

LHD I should not have gone to my local garden shop on that particular day. I had not slept well the night before, and I awoke tired, headachy, and out of sorts. I also had many other errands that needed doing that day. Yet the weather was beautiful, spring had come, and it was time to purchase bedding plants and supplies.

Arriving at the store I parked near where the peat moss, manure, and other planting essentials are kept. The gardening shop was extremely busy, with people everywhere. I entered and quickly filled my buggy with pink, lavender, and orange impatiens. I planted impatiens every year and by now I had it down to a science: this much peat moss, this much root stimulator, this much composted manure. As I stood in the line, a small blond man entered the store and saw someone he knew. He told his friend, chuckling, "Can't go home without that red mulch." He got in line behind me. I checked out and headed to my car to get someone to load the bags that I had purchased.

I sat restlessly in my car for at least fifteen minutes as the yard men loaded someone else. Then I pulled up closer. I saw the small blond man get in his car and pull up a few seconds later. He got out of his car. I got out of my car. The yard man approached and said, "I'll load you up as soon as I get this guy." He pointed to the short blond man.

"No, that's not right," I said. "I was here before him. He just got out of his car first. I was waiting."

"Sir," the yard man said to the blond man, "can I load up this lady now?"

The blond man insisted that *he* was first. I flushed with anger. The good angel on my shoulder was shouting at me, "It doesn't matter! Just wait! Calm down!"

But I didn't listen. "You were not here first; you just got out of your car first," I said to the blond man firmly. He shook his head at me, and raising his voice said, "Yes, I was next!" And I lost the battle. I sat in my car and seethed. Now the yard man and the blond man were chatting and laughing together. Were they speaking about how difficult we women shoppers are? I got out of my car again.

"Excuse me! I see you have time to chat now? What about my order? I want you to know I was checking out when that man entered your store!" I jabbed my finger toward him. The blond man looked at me angrily, shaking his head, and I wanted to throw something at him. The yard man said that he was waiting on the forklift. Now *he* was looking at me in a strange way. I could not believe I was acting like this. The good angel had given up her perch on my shoulder and flown to parts unknown, probably hiding behind the stacked clay pots in embarrassment. I had ignored her because I wanted to. I had been wronged. I was angry, and I wanted justice. I wanted some respect!

Finally, it was my turn, and I got loaded up. The yard man looked distressed and sad. He was a handsome young guy, probably a university student working on the weekend. I was still angry, and I showed it in my stony silence. I said an icy "thank you" through clenched teeth.

I drove my car out and headed downtown for the many errands I still had to do. My inner voice said, "What just happened here?"

I answered, "I don't know. I can't believe that I acted like that. It was an out of body experience. I felt so disrespected. But why? The employee was probably doing the best that he could. Still I'm upset." My head was pounding.

My inner voice began to probe: "Ah, Lyn Doucet, spiritual director, enlightened one. Didn't you say that your main goal, spiritually, was to add to the compassion of the world? Well, that wasn't it! Do you realize that you were about to go to fisticuffs with a man in a parking lot over peat moss. Good grief!"

I pulled into Dairy Queen and ordered a large Coke float, obviously hoping that sugar would help clear my head. I sat and pondered. As much as I tried to justify myself, I couldn't. It hadn't mattered who was first. Ten more minutes of my time would not have changed my day, and even if it had, so what? I was now taking time to soothe my nerves with highly refined carbohydrates, so obviously time was not the real issue. No, the truth was that I had wanted justice, but I had forgotten about mercy. And what about those gifts of the Spirit, like patience?

Mercy. That is what I wanted to embody. Mercy and compassion. My pride had gotten injured, and my sense of right violated on a day when I was vulnerable to the temptation of acting out in anger. Pride and self-righteousness are just what causes much of the violence in the world. Today peat moss, tomorrow other acts of aggression, anger, and revenge.

As I swirled the ice cream into the Coke with my straw, I saw clearly that prayer that does not transfer into expressed love is useless. One's heart must be changed, and one's actions too. I had to be careful, lest my prayer become mere piety. I would be the cup washed white on the outside, but filled with refuse on the inside.

I had to face it squarely: I led a wealthy and privileged life compared to most of the world. Patience should come easily to one so blessed, yet the very luxury of my life can have an opposite effect. I would go so far as to say I am spoiled by my easy access to everything I need and most of what I want, including instantly blooming flower beds. I certainly didn't relish thinking of myself as spoiled and demanding, but it was darkness that obviously existed within me.

After my enlightenment that day, I resolved that it would be a long time before I went to large, busy stores when I was not feeling well. I wouldn't pile so many things to do on my own head. I wouldn't lead myself into temptation in that way, for I recognized, once again, that pushing myself too hard leads to my being hard on others. Through small things, I learned important lessons.

When I told the story of the Great Peat Moss Battle to one of my dearest friends, Teenie, I was able to laugh at my foolishness. Teenie said, "Oh, Lyn, that's not like you at all."

I said smiling, "Yes, it is. I can be like that. And it can sneak up on me. I used to want to change the world, but now I struggle just to change *me* a little."

I confessed to Teenie that I probably should find the yard guy and apologize, but I wasn't going to. I was too embarrassed. In fact, I probably wouldn't go back to the garden store this season at all!

She smiled, and we split a Ground Patti hamburger with extra cheese and mushrooms. And she told me then that if I needed anything from that store in the near future, she'd pick it up for me.

Now that's mercy.   —L.H.D.

⚜ *Prayer for Forgiveness* ⚜

God, all knowing one,
You understand me better than I do myself.
You see the darkness within me, you know its source.
Shine the light of your grace upon it. Let me see myself
*   as others*
See me. As much as I can now, Dear Abba.
*   Jesus, Brother,*
You know my pride,
And sometimes it serves the world,
But not that often.
Help me to deal with it.
Don't let me forget that I can be as I would not,

Treating others as stair steps as I rise to grasp
My endless goals. With a heart
Darkened by greed and the desire for more, always
    more.
Heal that within me, moment by moment.
    Mother Wisdom, Enlivening Spirit,
You have been with sages and seers throughout the ages,
Be with me now.
Soften the urge within me to make myself right,
To seek justice for myself at the expense of others,
When just a little kindness and understanding,
And ah . . . gratitude,
Would ease the way.
    For is it not wisdom to walk in forgiveness?
To put down rancor,
And to resolve once again to travel lightly with patience,
    compassion, and joy.

Amen.

❧ Opening the Mind to God's Peaceful, Healing Presence ❧

Whoever becomes humble like this child is the greatest in the
kingdom of heaven.   —Matthew 18:4 NRSV

Jesus was constantly trying to teach his disciples to wake up,
to drop their preconceived ideas and to see things in a dif-
ferent way. Spiritual teachers throughout the ages have said

the same thing: "You're asleep! Become a beginner. Adopt the seeing of a child. That which you think you know, you do not."

Driven by a deeply ingrained cultural consciousness, we are so often buzzing about our days without seeing, without being aware of our motivations, of our inner driving voices. Our encounters with others become agenda-driven, and we miss so many of the gifts and the meaning of our days.

Compare this way of being to that of healthy children as they play and enjoy their world. They are fully present in the moment and open to whatever comes next. They are filled with wonder.

I have found the following simple exercises helpful and even enjoyable as I seek to become more awake and aware in the moment.

1. Suspending Disbelief

When you rise one morning, tell yourself that everyone you meet on this particular day has been put in your path for an important reason. Your life is a wonderful, dramatic mystery unfolding moment by moment, like a play upon a stage. Resolve on this one day to listen very carefully to everyone you meet and to look at that person closely in order to receive the messages people are bringing you. Try to speak less and to listen more. Quiet your mind chatter and enter fully into the moment of encounter with each person.

2. Really Seeing

Choose some living thing in your environment: your sleeping cat, a tree in your yard, a flower. Quiet your mind and *spend at least ten to fifteen minutes really looking at this living thing as you breathe quietly. Try to clear your head of language. Don't talk to yourself or say things such as: "This is a Floribunda rose and it is vulnerable to mold." This is the sort of labeling we want to avoid. Just observe quietly, as though you've never seen this thing before and know nothing about it. Really try to see in a peaceful and deeply felt way.*

3. The Wise Watcher

To practice more mindfulness, begin to observe yourself in love as you go through your days. Try not to judge and criticize yourself, but just pay attention. As author Eckhart Tolle says, there is a watcher within each of us, a wiser, eternal part of us that transcends our driven, competitive, sometimes violent cultural consciousness. Allow that watcher within you to begin to inform the rest of you. As you quiet the constant chatter of your mind, tune in to what is eternal, peace-filled, and life-giving within your own heart. Open your eyes to God and the wonder of life in each moment.

Walk in peace.

Help Me to Rest in You

Sabbath is a way of being in time where we remember who we are, remember what we know, and taste the gifts of spirit and eternity.
— Wayne Muller, *Sabbath: Restoring the Sacred Rhythm of Rest*

So God blessed the seventh day and hallowed it, because on it God rested from all the work that he had done in creation.
— Genesis 2:3 NRSV

RH I took my first tennis lessons last summer. I have never professed to be a good athlete, but my new and much more athletic husband and I agreed that a few lessons might allow me to return a few balls, giving us some shared exercise. I did, in fact, learn a little about the game, enough to keep score and deliver a few return shots within bounds. But I learned something else very valuable: the *resting posture,* the position between shots in which you stand in relaxed readiness, with the racket resting lightly in your hands. No grip. Just resting. The results of the posture were immediately evident, even in my feeble game. I seemed to have more focus and power on the return shot, whereas if I stayed intense the entire game, I simply wore myself out. And so it is with life, too.

We Americans, especially, have forgotten the necessity of rest. I watched a segment on *CBS This Morning* a few years ago about a new trend in family vacations. It showed a family going to the beach for a week. In their tote were a pager, a cell phone, even a laptop computer! While Mom was on the beach enjoying the kids, the sun, and the sand, Dad was inside the condo connected to the office. I was so saddened for this family and for any of us that choose to be that "wired" to the world, overly accessible through our cell phones, computers, and myriad other hi-tech tools of communication. Too much grip. Not enough rest.

Wayne Muller states powerfully, "The world aches for the generosity of well-rested people." God knew the necessity of rest at the time of creation, for *he* even rested, later commanding us to keep the Sabbath as well. Yet, Sabbath isn't just an obligation to meet. As Muller explains, "Sabbath is more than the absence of work; it is not just a day off when we catch up on television or errands. It is the presence of something that arises when we consecrate a period of time to listen to what is most deeply beautiful, nourishing, or true."

I have been learning just how far I have yet to go to truly honor the Sabbath as God intended, but I have also received many benefits from my efforts to utilize this sort of sacred resting posture. When I truly consecrate time to listen to God, an energy wells up from my center that anchors me in a complete feeling of security. I am at ease and often in awe. There is no hunger, for I am simply *full*. Gratitude becomes an energy that exudes from my being. I rest better and worry less. Mostly, I become tuned in to synchronicity, beauty, nature, loving, goodness, and even the virtues of those I love. I am filled with God's light, so I can more fully offer light to others.

From a mountain cabin in Dillsboro, North Carolina, the first day of a recent week-long vacation in the Blue Ridge Mountains,

I wrote the following thoughts: "No phone or television for a week! How awesome to have this time to detoxify from the whims of the world. Already, the patches of pink, yellow, and violet wildflowers that dot the mountainside lift my spirit. The fresh honeysuckled mountain air fills my soul, reminding me of those necessary times in my life — daily, weekly, monthly, and now yearly — when I must stop and smell the roses. Literally."

But one doesn't need a wildflower-strewn mountainside, gurgling brook, pristine beach, or even the sacred space of a favorite retreat center to enter Sabbath time. A comfortable living room chair, porch swing, or spot in the garden will do. And while I do believe that we need a week or so, occasionally, to cleanse ourselves from our everyday world, we also need time *daily* in the ordinary rhythm of our day to step back, exhale, and breathe in God's goodness. The important thing is that we claim it and then use that time to become more sensitive to the ways God loves us, more in tune with his tender guidance. During Sabbath, the focus is on God — his beauty, his love, his grace, and his comfort. We yield our precious time to God, trusting that he will fill it with himself, that which is, without question, the most beautiful, nourishing, and true.   — R.H.

Change and Heal Me, God

Embracing the mystery of depression does not mean passivity or resignation. It means moving into a field of forces that seems alien but is in fact one's deepest self. It means waiting, watching, listening and suffering, and gathering whatever self knowledge one can — One begins the slow walk by choosing each day things that enliven one's selfhood and resisting things that do not.
—Parker Palmer, *Let Your Life Speak*

LHD On the second Sunday of Lent at St. Joseph Church in the village of Milton, Louisiana, I entered the sanctuary quickly, almost late. I knelt near the choir and began to pray, still grappling with a strange feathery darkness that had settled around my heart. I wasn't sure what had caused it. A winter that had gone on too long, with me sequestered with writing and terrible news of war on television? A cold that wouldn't quite go away? Loneliness? The physical changes of midlife? My usual demons: the critical inner voices that were never satisfied? I didn't know. But I was tired of the darkness, weary with it. Desolation had come into my life and my prayer.

As Fr. Keith in purple robes led a solemn procession of altar servers and readers down the aisle, the choir began a haunting refrain: "Hold us in your mercy; hold us in your mercy." "I will be able to pray deeply today," I thought. "I have no music responsibilities; I can just be here now, lifting my voice." I

111

squeezed my eyes shut, praying with the refrain, "Hold us in your mercy; hold us in your mercy." I thought of the ways I that I failed and entered deeply into the chant which now changed to "Kyrie eleison, Christi eleison." Suddenly I felt a hand on my shoulder: "Can you manage two folks in here?" an usher asked me. I came back from miles away. Ah, now I remembered; Mass was a community celebration. A handsome couple in their twenties settled in, smiling apologetically.

The readings began. Abram had fallen into a frightening darkness just before God appeared in smoke and fire, sealing the Hebrew covenant. I thought of my own darkness. What promises of God might be revealed in my small suffering? Rich chords began to sound on the organ as the cantor intoned, "The Lord is my light and my salvation."

As the readings continued, St. Paul's Letter to the Philippians advised listeners to stand firm and to turn away from shame. My depression felt like shame; it felt like failure. I listened as Paul exhorted all to raise their minds from earthly things and to consider citizenship in heaven, where lowly bodies will be glorified. My mind resisted any images of heaven, held firmly to earth by the shadows around my heart, but I considered what it means to "stand firm in the Lord." Perhaps this was what I was doing by being in church when I didn't feel like being there.

Then Fr. Keith read the Gospel recounting of Jesus' ascent of Mount Tabor, where he was lit and transfigured by God's glorious light. This was an incredible mountaintop experience for the disciples, who wanted to remain there in the sacred light. But even this glorious moment took place in the looming shadow of the cross as Jesus knew the suffering that was to come. This reality was missed by the disciples, who wished to remain atop the mountain continually bathed in the light. I was like those disciples; I wanted only mountaintops, joy, and lightness of being. I had a momentary vision of myself picketing heaven: "Give us light and only light!" my sign read. I smiled to myself. Ah, I was deeply hungry for light today and so I was listening, really listening. As I was touched by each of the readings, I thought, "We are shaped by darkness and light and this is the way it must be." I tried to put down my imaginary picketing sign and my questions, to stop my resistance to an immersion in mystery.

Across the aisle, an elfin face engaged mine. Sophie, a wonderful little girl of five whom I know, gazed at me as though we shared a secret. She tilted her small head knowingly. "What is it?" I pondered. What did the little girl think of all these words, this singing and reading? Suddenly I knew something clearly: We are becoming. The thought was crystal clear: We are always in the process of changing and becoming what we will be. Sophie would grow in mysterious ways, nourished by her faith and many other things, and I would grow also. We would grow together through darkness and light. The desolation that I felt was a part of this growth. I didn't like it, but somehow it had to be this way. Ah, and then there was Jesus as Eucharist, held high by the priest, broken, broken, broken. Broken for our brokenness. And God could not even spare his son from being broken by darkness.

And though I usually didn't do this, today, during the Lamb of God, I humbly touched my heart. With each repetition of "Lamb of God, you take away the sin of the world, have mercy on us," I touched my own heart gently with love and forgiveness as if to massage it tenderly. As I patted my heart I did something else I rarely do: I prayed very specifically for myself.

"God, I am sad and I want to feel better. If it is your will, lift the darkness from my heart." As I finished my prayer, I said with the congregation, "Grant us peace."

Ah, and then there was Jesus as Eucharist, held high by the priest, broken, broken, broken. Broken for our brokenness. And God could not even spare his son from being broken by darkness.

A purple banner swung peacefully over my head, stirred by the air conditioning. To my right and high above me, golden light streamed through a brilliantly colored, round stained-glass window. I was mildly stunned when the choir began to sing, "We shall be changed! The trumpet will sound! The dead will be raised. And we shall be changed!" I looked at Linda, a dark-haired librarian from the university who was singing as though she really believed; she was singing with all her heart. Five choir members played bells, acrobatically switching from one bell to another, their eyes glued to the chord chart in front of them. They were lost in sweet service as a high descant began, weaving into the melody, wafting toward heaven. I too was now singing with feeling, "We shall be changed! Yes, we shall be changed!"

Sophie nodded her pixie head at me, singing just a little, her little chin dipping. Was I Sophie? Was she the child that I was? She turned back the other direction and her shiny dark brown hair swung with her movements; her young life filled me.

We are changing and becoming, I thought. Let it be. Let me be able to just watch, listen, and accept, just going along with what is.

As the choir received Communion many of them smiled at me. When the service ended, Sophie waved and ran to the gathering area to get a donut, with her pink and white apron dress swishing above her lacy white socks and black patent leather shoes. I collected as many hugs as I could from friends who were coming by. I lingered to chat, and in those very few moments I heard about lost jobs, pending divorces, homes that had to be sold. I didn't beat myself up because my problems were mild or hard to pin down; I just listened.

Outside, winter was ending. The azaleas were offering their fuchsia flowers at the church door. Hope. The birds were in a havoc of joy. I didn't know when my own desolation would leave completely, but as I walked to my car, I repeated a sweet mantra: *We shall be changed.* —L.H.D.

⤚ *Desolation in Prayer* ⤙

All we know of being is becoming. Being alive, being grateful, means becoming alive, becoming grateful. Being human means becoming what we are. If you stopped becoming, you would cease to be. Yet, in the process of becoming you cease to be what you were.... [Therefore] fullness and emptiness are inextricably one.
—David Steindl-Rast, *Gratefulness, the Heart of Prayer*

The action of the evil spirit upon souls is violent, noisy, and disturbing. It can be compared to a drop of water falling upon a stone.... The evil one gradually attempted to make one step down from the state of spiritual delight and joy.
—St. Ignatius of Loyola, *The Spiritual Exercises*

Periods of desolation in prayer are marked by emptiness, by a feeling that God is far away and is indifferent to our suffering. We have stepped down from heights of delight and joy in

*prayer. As our lives and our hearts change, we seem to be try-
ing to reach a God who seems unreachable. Instead of being
lifted by hope and gratitude, we are drawn into darkness and
may question our faith. We are tempted to withdraw from
community of any sort.*

*Through the centuries, writers have asked what causes
desolation in prayer. Such periods seem to be a time of pu-
rification when we are asked to seek God for God alone, and
not for the warm feelings that may come to us in prayer. Desolation is often a time of testing, when our motives and goals
come to light. Sometimes we see that we have tried to add
God on as a spiritual treasure, adding him on to all the other
things that drive us, rather than putting God first in our lives.*

*During desolation, it is important to do four things: First,
distinguish desolation from depression, which can be dangerous to a person's long-term well-being. While desolation may
have some of the symptoms of depression, such as low vitality
and darkness, a person in a state of clinical depression will
often stop eating or sleeping well or will eat and sleep too
much. An overall agitation and very deep hopelessness occurs for the depressed person, and even thoughts of suicide.
Depression is a time to seek medical help.*

*Second, during a time of spiritual desolation we should
avoid making major changes or decisions, especially those
that draw us away from God, like leaving a small-faith
community because of feelings of alienation. It is a time to
persevere in seeking God in community as well as through
prayer and in these ways resist the influence of evil forces in
our spirits.*

Third, keep a record of times of consolation: prayers answered, deep satisfaction in prayer, times we felt the warmth of God's love, in order to be able to return to these rich memories and to instill ourselves with hope. For this is one reason, among many others, that journaling is important.

Finally, we should seek out a listening ear, be it a vowed religious, a spiritual director, or a good friend who can be counted on just to listen. Desolation flourishes when a person is isolated. It is often hard to reach out to others, but it is very important to do so during desolation.

Remember that periods of desolation do end and that God is present to us at all times. Sometimes we cannot perceive this presence. Yet God's unconditional love never fails.

Thank You, Father, with All My Heart

Shame kills intimacy. The soul that still is in some way hiding cannot enjoy the fullness of knowing what characterizes the love between God and the saints in heaven.
—Brent Curtis and John Eldredge, *The Sacred Romance*

I give you thanks, O Lord, with my whole heart.... On the day I called, you answered me, you increased my strength of soul.
—Psalm 138:1, 3 NRSV

RH I was sitting contentedly on my mom's bed playing with my new grandson when my mother suddenly disappeared into her closet, returning with a lockbox I'd never seen before. Almost sacramentally, she placed it on her bed, explaining to me that there was something she kept forgetting that she wanted to give me. Shuffling through papers and the sentimental treasures contained in the box, she reverently placed in my hands a tattered, water-stained picture of a chubby-faced little schoolgirl. I felt confused and awed, as Mamma explained to me that this was the photograph of me that my daddy had carried in his wallet, the very one he had with him when, on an ominous day in 1964, the airplane he was traveling on crashed into Lake Pontchartrain.

I had no idea that this particular picture existed. I had heard stories of the wallet, the only tangible possession of his that was recovered from the lake. The brown leather object had served to force my little ten-year-old mind out of denial and into the reality that Daddy had in fact been on the plane that day and wouldn't show up somewhere some place in the distant future with amnesia or something. But I knew that the wallet had been stolen from its storage place in Daddy's chest of drawers stowed in my sister's garage. I guess I had presumed that its contents had also been taken.

I held the photograph in my hands, and in my heart embraced a feeling of connection to Daddy. I don't think I had ever wondered whether he carried my picture with him. Suddenly, I felt so special! A feeling of love and belonging surged up within me. Glancing at the innocent face of this nine-year-old with the braided hair and short brown bangs, the smiling image of a child who up to that point lived in a secure and protected world, I felt sad for what she didn't yet know. Memories of the event thirty-eight years ago that would change my life forever flooded my heart. I knew it was no accident that the picture had appeared at that moment in time, but found it odd that Mamma had never before remembered to give it to me. Or *was* it odd? In two days, I was scheduled to begin a five-day, private, directed retreat at the Teresian Sisters Provincialate in Covington, Louisiana.

I've always known that the healing of memories is a lifelong process, a sort of peeling away the layers of an onion. I liken the pain to shrapnel in a wound never cleaned out completely, which throbs only on occasion, with the change of weather perhaps. I could feel my spiritual weather changing as I reverently taped the picture in my journal. My retreat had begun.

ENTERING THE RETREAT HOUSE, I was a bit uneasy with the unfamiliar environment. There wasn't a soul around. Well, not exactly. A little plaque hanging unassumingly on the wall caught my eye, and I could sense the spirit of St. Teresa of Avila beckoning my first prayer. The words inscribed on the plaque were hers: "He speaks clearly to our hearts when we beg him from our hearts to do so." My heart was ready to be spoken to as I whispered under my breath, "Speak, Lord, your servant is listening," marking my willingness to embrace whatever God had in store for me. How comforting to later discover that the sisters living on the property would be praying for me throughout my five days. I would never see much of their community, but feeling their kindred spirits and their yearning for my complete acceptance of God's grace over the next five days nurtured my soul into openness and receptivity.

During my initial meeting with my director, Sr. Gloria, I was offered the marvelous consolation that God was inviting me to receive more of him. I inscribed my response in my journal: "Lord, help me to accept what you have to give me, to be able to relax and to open my heart completely." She assigned four Scripture passages for my first day of prayer and assured me that her own and the sisters' prayers for me would continue.

I began my first prayer period with the words of Isaiah from chapter 54 that Sister had suggested. I could hear the wisdom of the prophet bidding my openness to healing: "The shame of your youth you shall forget." Glancing with love at the prized photograph, I sensed the shame under my timid smile. I had struggled all my life with feelings of inferiority, and after Daddy's death, I always felt so different from others, and incomplete. I seemed to be overly vulnerable, always searching outside of myself for value, protection, and fatherly care. To make matters worse, I always expected the inevitable. No matter how secure or loved I felt in any moment, it seemed it couldn't last.

God, too, was someone I couldn't count on always. His presence, though becoming much more loving, was also fleeting. I felt him very near to me, then, as I earnestly prayed, "I hear you tell me to put my shame behind me, that you are my help and therefore I am not disgraced. I see you calling me to a knowing that you will never leave me, no matter what." Sr. Gloria had prompted me to ask God for help in letting go, so he might enter, so that my trust in him could build. My heartfelt prayer continued: *Help me to relax, O God.*

Over the next several days, God's marvelous creations became my comfort: the sweet birdsong, the cool spring breeze, the iridescent sunrises in the window over my bed, the view from my room of the nearby rose bed flourishing with color, and even the chubby little nun shooing the cat from the garden. One morning sitting on my bed in prayer, I glanced at these words from Psalm 62: "God alone is my rock and my salvation, my secure height; I shall not fall." It seemed so easy to trust God in the confines of this pristine environment.

By midweek I had relaxed completely into my sacred space and daily rhythm of prayer. I had become accustomed to finding my food in the kitchen each day, set out as if by little elves, and then sharing my meals in silence with one other retreatant. Each day I walked for miles, exploring the pine tree-strewn landscape and attending Mass at nearby monasteries. Every homily, bearing themes of humility and childlike trust, further adorned my retreat. The angelic voices of the cloistered Carmelites from the hidden chamber of their chapel down the road echoed the voices of heaven. I felt so open.

Then one evening in prayer sitting alone in the chapel, there it was in the very midst of my openness: the *wall*, the fortress I had constructed around my heart to protect myself from pain, the pseudo-security I had erected to insulate myself from hurt and abandonment, disappointment and fear. I encountered it by surprise, sitting in that silent, sacred space. Even here, this barrier was firmly in place, keeping me from the God I thought I trusted.

Questions erupted from a deeper place inside that needed no safeguarding, the place within that was trusting and free of concern about what the answers might be: Lord, I know this wall has protected me from those who have hurt me, but why from you? Am I afraid, Lord, even of you? Am I fearful to empty myself completely, to tear down the false self that this wall seemingly protects? Am I afraid to grow up completely and sur- render my clinging nature? Or am I just fearful of giving up the control hidden by this invisible but deadly façade of protection?

It was deeply painful to admit to myself how impoverished my life was at times by my need to protect my heart, how much I had sacrificed my true self — a self that was free to love and be loved. I had so often exchanged my most genuine nature for a false sense of security. I wanted so much more. I prayed longingly, "Help me, Lord, to let you all the way in, to break down my barriers and to penetrate fully my defenses. I want *you* to be my protection, my refuge, my fortress, safety, and hope. I do want to open my heart completely."

In response, it seemed as if God invited me to just rest in him.

The following morning, determined to let God all the way in, I continued my earnest effort to open myself up. I humbly thanked him for his patience and, mostly, for his love, even when I couldn't seem to let go enough to let it in. I asked him to help me surrender *even this desire* to be close to him. I heard God say, "Be quieter still. Listen, and just be." Grace began to encase my spirit like a soft fleece blanket.

The next several hours were the most restful and peaceful of my life, as God tenderly whispered, "Be still and know that I am God. Be still. Be still..." In a grace-filled stupor, I felt like an infant swaddled and snuggled in his love. As if in his very arms, I rested for hours, gazing, napping, taking in the beautiful sunshine and the cool May breeze. The sense of comfort was truly womb-like. Love penetrated my defenses. I couldn't seem to move. I didn't want to. I was held by Love. What more could I want? In those prayerful hours, there was no wall, no shame. Just openness, freedom, joy, and deep abiding peace in the center of my being.

As I spoke of my experience of such penetrating love with Sr. Gloria hours later, I shared my discovery that the Fathering I had sought all my life had always been there. I had been bathed in God's love, a love that had been there from the very beginning of my existence. I realized that even the wall around my heart had, in a sense, been a grace, a kind of pseudo-fathering that I had used to protect me as a father should. But it was no longer needed. My desperate search for protection had at last ended in the arms of the one, true Father of us all.

Thumbing back many pages in my journal to glance once more at the cherished photograph of that little girl, I wrote my final prayer of the retreat. It seemed to articulate for both that child and the woman she had become the profound inner healing that had occurred over my five prayerful days:

Precious Lord,

Thank you for calling me here and back to you to be your loving daughter. All my life I have yearned for a father. I sought him in a daddy, a stepfather, a husband. You were certainly present in all of them, but I clung to them even when they abandoned me. I became the selfish, narcissistic child, seeking constant care and solace that couldn't possibly be provided by anyone but you.

You, Father, originator and source of my life, have fathered me from the beginning. You knit me in my mother's womb, called me forth by name, and provided eternal love for me. Love that always was and always will be. You were there for me in my greatest struggles and have taken care of me and tended to all of my needs. You have found favor with me, because I am your daughter. How lucky I am!

Thank you, Lord, Father, for your invitation this week to be still, to listen to your whispers, and mostly to trust my life in your care. Thank you for it all and for your priceless presence. Amen.

—R.H.

Why Go on Retreat?

A retreat is an opportunity to allow God to heal, transform, and re-create one's very soul. It offers the sacred time of extended prayer and fasting from busyness and shallow living, a quiet break in one's hectic life for deep reflection and response to God's presence. A retreat is an extended Sabbath.

Like anything else, retreats come in all shapes and sizes. There are preached retreats, presented by a qualified retreat director, that encompass a theme and follow a series of talks that are presented throughout the day. These retreats normally last a few days and are often, but not always, silent.

Between the talks, retreatants are on their own to dwell in prayer, to rest, walk, journal, or engage in whatever quiet activities they feel led to. Lyn and I have given retreats of this kind and find them to be most helpful especially, though not always, for beginners.

A private directed retreat, like the one described in the previous essay, is a personally guided prayer experience that can last for three to as long as thirty days. Each retreatant is assigned a director with whom the retreatant meets daily for reflection and spiritual discernment. Several Scripture passages are assigned each day followed by personal time spent in prayer, listening, rest, and leisure. Often incorporated into these retreats are the Spiritual Exercises of St. Ignatius of Loyola, adapted according to the disposition and spiritual background of the individual retreatant.

It is daunting for some to consider going on retreat. Leaving one's familiar spaces and venturing into the unknown to be with strangers for several days seems too much to contemplate. But for those who are serious about the spiritual journey, an annual retreat is almost a must.

These are some things retreats have done for us:

1. *The retreat has been time alone with God without any other responsibilities. This has provided ample time to look at our relationship with God, with others, and with ourselves, sometimes addressing inner pain and wounds.*

2. *We now understand the wisdom of silence while on retreat. The world we live in can be noisy, overly busy, and chaotic. It is difficult to have a relationship with God without experiencing exterior and interior silence. We*

*both have learned to seek silence in everyday life, silence
that helps us stay prayerful.*

3. *We have been inspired by fellow retreatants, presenters,
   directors, and others who are living a God-centered life,
   by their courage, wisdom, and willingness to share their
   experiences. We have learned to develop deep intimacy
   with others through retreat experiences, even while sharing meals together in silence. The ordinary ways we are
   judged in our culture fall away on retreats. Our value is
   not determined by our appearance, wealth, or jobs. We
   become naked souls seeking God together.*

4. *We have reveled in the beauty of the natural world during
   retreats. Many retreat houses take special care in providing their guests with beautiful surroundings. This peaceful
   enjoyment of nature has strengthened our relationships
   with our Creator, making us deeply grateful for the created world. This gratitude and enjoyment carry over into
   everyday life.*

5. *We have listened deeply to our inner voices on retreat and
   practiced discernment about career and family issues. We
   have done important dream work.*

6. *We have increased our knowledge and experience of spirituality many times over through talks from wonderful
   writers and presenters, group experiences, and recom-
   mended reading done with a quiet heart.*

7. *Retreats can be fun and relaxing when one is stressed and
   overworked. There is often wholesome laughter, and it is
   wonderful not to have to prepare meals, clean house, or*

even answer the phone for a few days. Although for some, being away from cell phones can be taxing, freedom from interruptions is an essential part of this journey.

The following are just a few websites with wonderful information about finding a retreat center:

- *www.osb.org/retreats*
- *www.jesuit.org/sections (click on resources)*
- *www.spiritsite.com/centers*

Take an opportunity to do some research on the Internet or ask friends in your church and community where you might go on retreat. You might be amazed at the wonderful speakers and writers who are coming into your area. There may be orders of religious near you who offer various kinds of retreats. Take a little risk and do something different. You can carve out the time for this if you plan ahead. Attending a retreat will enrich your life and deepen your faith walk more than you can imagine.

Burning with Your Love

Leaning with nothing to lean on
Without light and in darkness
I go burning with love.
Of Love, I have had experience,
Of the good, of the bad that it finds in me
It know how to benefit (what power)
It changes my soul into itself.
— Jean Chalon, *Thérèse of Lisieux:*
A Life of Love

LHD The sun was hot on my shoulders, as I reached down through the leaves of a tomato plant to pluck the fruit. The tomato was warm in my hand, red-ripe and filled to bursting with juice. I placed it in the oaken egg basket that a friend had made for me. I had picked from only one plant, and already the basket was full.

As I picked, my mind was full of the little one, Thérèse of Lisieux. I had been rereading her autobiography and various books about her. Her first jobs at the convent were to sweep the porches, fill the water pitchers, and see to a certain elderly nun who needed help to go from place to place. Thérèse, who had probably never touched a broom before her novitiate, was castigated for missing a cobweb and was told that her filling of pitchers was hasty and sloppy. The old nun for whom she cared was cantankerous and ungrateful. Nothing Thérèse did anywhere in the convent was quite right. Plagued with stomach problems from the rough food and tortured by all the disdain, she fought depression and doubt. This vocation was to be her path: the subjugation of a rich and passionate nature, a kind of death. And yet under all the self-denial and the pain burned . . . fire.

I carried the ripe tomatoes into the kitchen and began washing and cutting them up for canning. My kitchen sink reflected their shining redness, and as they cooked, their zesty aroma filled the air. I simmered onions. I added salt and a little sugar, and everything bubbled happily on top of my stove. I recalled that Thérèse loved the things of summer, like the fruit of my tomato vines. During her years in the convent she watched for the flowers of her childhood and rejoiced when she found even one. As a petted and carefree child she had played in the gardens of her home, picking wildflowers and caring for the rabbits in their cages. She loved all living things, for they spoke to her of the God she loved most. Entering the Carmelite monastery at only fifteen years of age, she embraced suffering. Separated from her beloved father and sorely tested by her superiors, she experienced extensive internal darkness of spirit. During that time she courageously wrote:

> And so I fear nothing, neither sword nor flame
> No, nothing can trouble my ineffable peace
> And the fire of the love that consumes my soul
> Will never go out!

In those sultry days of summer, I had been inspired by the Little Flower and her interior fire. Little that appeared on the outside indicated such great passion within her. She lived humbly in the Carmel and tried valiantly to please those with whom she lived. She maintained a cheerful and pleasant exterior under extreme duress. There was class envy in the convent, and in particular of the four Martin sisters who lived there. Her superiors, seeing her wonderful soul, felt it their duty to test her by adversity, a young girl who longed for their motherly love. They forced her to bank her passion down, so low that it seemed to be gone, but it only grew in the darkness, her great darkness.

I smiled with affection for her as I turned the heat down under the tomatoes. I placed four jars in hot water and thumbed through the book that I had been rereading the night before, Jean Chalon's *Thérèse of Lisieux: A Life of Love.* Poor little thing, I thought now. I felt motherly toward her.

So young. Yes, she embraced the life in the cloister, but was it to be near her sisters after the death of their mother? Was this the only life she could visualize? Then she was struck down so young with tuberculosis, a disease that today can be cured with antibiotics but was often fatal then. She was only twenty-four when she died. How long would she have lived if she had been born at a different time? What else would she have learned, have said, have written? And yet, and yet.... Here I was so many years later and her words simmered within me as my tomatoes simmered on the stove. Odd, the workings of Grace. For as Thérèse lay dying so young, her passionate fire burst forth unabated. She burned. She blazed. She vowed to be a force of heaven as she grasped immortality with fiery hands.

And on this August day she had led me to touch the fire in my soul also, the fire of the eternal creation, the starry remnants of the big bang. On that morning in my kitchen, I felt a fire that connects all being; as Gerard Manley Hopkins says,

"The world is charged with the grandeur of God," a grandeur that shone in the watery sink of bobbing tomatoes, that bubbled red on my stove, that burned with pure life. I was led to ask, "Is this stove an altar today? Is this splattered counter a holy place? Is this kitchen the place where, even for a moment, I am transformed within?" For while I sometimes claim that my *work* is my prayer (and that is quite often a cop-out), at that moment I felt it as a reality of the heart. The act of cooking tomatoes was transformative, and within the bubbling blue-speckled pot, a sacred alchemy was occurring.

I finished filling my jars, wiped the sticky counters with deep peace and went to bed. I hoped to have an important dream about Thérèse, but I slept soundly, dreamlessly. Soon the morning light was filtering in through my window as my husband slept beside me. I propped myself up on pillows and gazed out the glass-fronted door onto our little porch. The trees were an intense blue-green, seen only in the depth of summer after much rain. Suddenly . . . a red flash. A cardinal swooped onto the little porch, wings fanned out, backlit by the rising sun . . . and there it was once again: *fire.*

Filled with simmering joy, I mused that despite all her hardships, Thérèse felt that the good Lord gave her every heart's desire. And deep within a hot Louisiana summer, this same good God desired to give me fiery tomatoes and cardinals and the words of a passionate young girl, words that burned their way into my heart and enlarged my vision once again. Heaven became not a place but a way of seeing. What could all this be but grace? Where could I be but the kingdom of heaven?   —L.H.D.

Hear My Mother-Heart

But while he was still far off, his father saw him and was filled with compassion; he ran and put his arms around him and kissed him.
—Luke 15:20b NRSV

Mothers have to let sons (and daughters) go so that they can find their home to the love of God. While sons are away, mothers are called to trust God with all their heart, soul, and strength.

They are called to pray long into the night.

—Carolyn Nabors Baker, *Caught in a Higher Love*

RH My son Michael was always such an inquisitive little fellow. He knew that I cherished his questions, so he often prefaced them with the statement "Mom, you're going to think this is a good question." Sometimes he wondered aloud where the birds and butterflies sleep, and one time he asked me what I wanted to be when I grew up. He was, and is, a tenderhearted guy who always seems to be seeking ways to relate to the world.

Michael was about six years old when he raised the question "What was the first thing that ever was?" While I was busy trying to figure out what he meant by his question, he was already thinking aloud and answering it himself. With great enthusiasm, he suddenly announced, "I know, it was dinosaurs! No, it must have been Adam and Eve!" And then with absolute clarity and a seeming inner awareness that he'd hit on the truth, he declared, "I know, Mom, the first thing in the world was *love!*"

I daresay we know more truth when we're young and untainted by a very complex, often unloving world. It's sad that somewhere along the way we lose our grasp of the simple realities that matter the most. To consider the idea that love was the first thing that ever was is to cherish the immensity and simplicity of ageless wisdom. We are told that God is Love and that God always was and always will be. Jesus gave loving as the greatest commandment. St. Thérèse said that the most important thing is that our hearts are free to love. Given such mandates and saintly role models, one would think it would be easy for all of us to simply love.

Michael is now nineteen, and I can say that loving my son seemed a tad simpler when he was six and not free to make some of the choices his mom would prefer he didn't make. In a recent conversation he initiated, he was struggling with our relationship, perhaps trying to reconcile some of the hurt he'd caused in the past. Knowing how different our interests and values are, yet desiring to find that mutual place where we could connect once again, he posed another Michael question: "But, Mom, how do we relate to one another when we don't have anything in common anymore?"

By grace, I told him that the one thing we share is the *only* thing we need, and that it is love. Knowing he loves me and that I love him and always will no matter what is all the connection we need. We both cried in that simple but powerful realization. I reminded him of his own youthful wisdom and consummate tender heart, as well as the many, many times I have been sure of his love.

The real test came only days later with an unexpected phone call informing me of trouble he'd gotten into with a college prank. I couldn't believe that once again I found myself in such painful turmoil regarding my son. Lying in bed that night in an angry stupor, I prayed for peace and trust. I was immediately graced with the image of the father of the prodigal son. Suddenly he seemed so real to me, as if we were old friends commiserating over our lost sons. As I reflected on his situation, I wondered what he did between the times that his son left and returned.

Sitting on the phone at my kitchen desk the next morning, I shared that question with my friend Neddie. She had called to ask for prayers for a mutual acquaintance whose grandson had died, a request that helped me to keep things in perspective. Neddie replied, "He probably sat with a cup of coffee in his hand and kept an eye on the back door." Smiling, I glanced at the cup of coffee I held, then over at the back door. Comforted by her wisdom, I felt some sense of reassurance, trusting that they all do, indeed, come home eventually.

As Michael did. In his hand-scrawled note in a recent Mother's Day card was an answer to every prayer I have ever muttered for my son, his words of love and gratitude profoundly expressing the tenderness in him I always faithfully believed in:

Mom,

We've come a long way. From afternoon naps when I was a little guy, to strolls down Memory Lane, to a long distance relationship. And now, my love for you is more than ever. There's not a day that goes by where I don't thank GOD for having you as my mom. You're such a special person, so strong, and so loving. . . . It feels like it's my time to give back to you. To give back those thousands

*of hugs and kisses, to somehow give back the love and sacrifice
you so willingly gave to me.*

*Your love means so much to me, it was your love that gave me
life. Mom, I love you so much, and I hope that every Mother's Day
gets more and more special and meaningful for you, because I'll
tell you something, it sure does for me!*

I love you. Michael

As I read the loving words my son wrote to me, they reminded
me of Paula D'Arcy's wisdom in *Seeking with All My Heart:* "Do
we sense the change that Love's power can bring about? . . . That
we will not be the same once it has enveloped us?" I realized
that this enveloping Love has changed both Michael and me. It
truly is the first thing that ever was.   —R.H.

I Am So Deeply Grateful

There is in all visible things an invisible fecundity, a dimmed light, a meek namelessness, a hidden wholeness. This mysterious unity and Integrity is Wisdom, the Mother of all, Natura naturens. . . . This is at once my own nature, and the Gift of my Creator's thought and Art.
— Thomas Merton, *Hagia Sophia: A Thomas Merton Reader*

Make a joyful noise to the Lord, all the lands! Serve the Lord with gladness! Come into his presence with singing!
— Psalm 100:1–2 NRSV

LHD I prayed on this day in gratitude. The day demanded it. I had zipped on my red hooded sweatshirt and stepped into a March day that was cool and bright. Spring had come, and I welcomed it with all my heart.

My husband, Dee, had mowed the front pasture, leaving clumps of clover blooming white, with just a touch of pink where the stems were attached. Purple vetch adorned the ditch — its rich color a pretty contrast to the tall, amber winter grasses. I took long strides out onto the shell drive. I was still coughing a little, but that was it: I refused to be sick anymore!

I breathed in thanks, I breathed out thanks. My beloved sky was filmed with a light fog that was being sipped away by the sun. We would have few clouds that day. The white shell underfoot was covered with brown leaves. When I first moved to south Louisiana I used to wonder why everyone had to rake and burn leaves in the *spring.* Now I knew that the new leaves on the live oaks were forcing the old ones off, a spiritual metaphor to be sure. This day our live oaks were shimmering, tender, new, yellow-green. The breeze was crisp, and I was grateful for my strong legs that could walk four miles, even after just recovering from my aggravating cold.

As I progressed on my walk, I saw that the pasture beside Slumberger Oil was filled with cattle in various shades of brown, all facing one way, munching on the new patches of dark green grass. Yellow bitterweed, its appearance so much prettier than its name, covered part of one field and it glowed in the sunlight. Dewberries were beginning to bloom already. Dee would be looking closely now and marking the spots where he could pick berries later. He loved fresh berries better than any food on earth besides boiled crawfish.

I remembered when my son, Jacques, was little and Dee would crush up the berries for him with sugar. Blackberry crush, they called it — not too original a name, but a delicious treat. I saw Jacques' little face in my mind now; lips and teeth stained purple, a big smile. I thought of blackberry cobbler too, my favorite. All gifts of the seasons. All the good fruit of God's earth. Mysterious unity and hidden wholeness.

As I turned up the road beside the park, I knew that I was in gratitude for another reason: my little flock of spiritual directees was doing well. There was Sarah, who was recovering from prescription drug addiction and had been drug free for five months. She was discovering an inner life that she had never dreamed existed. Her excitement about the new things she was learning had reignited my enthusiasm, and on her bad days, I was able to encourage her about how far God had led her out of darkness into new light. There was Jonathan, who had struggled for so long with alienation and anger. The healing he had experienced during this year was startling. An extremely talented person, he had begun to use his gifts in community and to open his heart to others. And there was Simone, a teacher with such an authentic faith that I stood in awe of its depth and vision. With Simone, I am a privileged listener, a fellow worshiper standing on holy ground. She has told me that God has rescued her, loved her, and kept her safe. She has told me that even her beautiful, enduring hope is his gift. "I haven't done any of it," she says.

Yes, they were doing well. And in the midst of my gratitude now an unsettling thought slipped in. Are my moods of desolation and consolation totally driven by circumstance? If so, where was my faith? Was I a blue sky Christian?

As I continued to walk, I mused that because of my state of consolation, I was able to extend to myself the kindness I easily gave to others. So I answered the inner critic: No, my faith is real. It is not perfect. It does not offer itself as all-knowing, as solving every problem of human existence on this side of heaven, but it is real and daily informs my life. I stopped and smiled. Ah, that inner critic always made me defensive. I breathed deeply, looking up at the clear turquoise sky, trying to think more gently.

I believed I knew now that all life was gift and that I was not entitled to any of it. I sought to embrace the meaning of the world's suffering as I exulted in the Love that had brought me this far along a sacred path. My prayers of gratitude were as real as my prayers of desolation. Somehow, everything belonged.

I was passing by an older widow's home now. She had been frail, I know. But her yard was an absolute blaze of azaleas that were taller than I was. I walked through a wonder-world of delicate shimmering color: lilac, hot pink, rose, hoping that she could still enjoy this amazing exuberance of color and form. The large old azaleas asked nothing from her now. They were nourished by the sun and rain and fed by the leaf-fall on the good, good earth.

Returning from my walk, I picked four of the brilliant yellow daffodils blooming beside my walk. Seeing them emerge was always a happy surprise. Ah, their life span was so short, and yet they were so alive! I looked closely at them; what were they? How did they come to be, with their silky, delicate layers, their bright yellow color almost orange as it emerged from the dark brown dirt? Br. Steindl-Rast says that to the grateful heart, every gift is surprising, and on some days, "Gratefulness says it all." Knocking the dirt off my feet, I entered my house to find a vase and to write everything down. I didn't want to forget the gifts of this day. —L.H.D.

◈ *Consolation in Prayer* ◈

I call it consolation when an interior movement is aroused in the soul, by which it is inflamed with love of its Creator and Lord.
—St. Ignatius of Loyola, *The Spiritual Exercises*

When the spiritual seeker is in a state of consolation, God seems near and the inner spirit is enlivened with the gifts of peace and compassion for self and others. The person often wants to do more for God because of an increase in faith and to spend more time in her community of believers. Consolation leads us outward.

Consolation in the spiritual sense is not necessarily happiness as we usually perceive it. I think of my friend Brenda, who received deep consolation on one of the saddest days of her life. As she attended her brother's funeral, she was suddenly aware of being lifted on a blanket of prayer. The many people who had assured her they were praying for her truly were praying. She felt God come close. Her heart experienced a peace that was outside of her circumstances.

St. Ignatius of Loyola advised those in consolation not to become puffed up, lest they decide that this grace is of their own doing. He always taught that consolation is a gift of grace and not a reward for our goodness. It is helpful, however, for us to write about our consolation so that we can return to our memories when darkness comes. During desolation, the memories of past graces received can lift us and give us hope.

Perhaps one of the most helpful things to know is that both consolation and desolation in prayer and in life come to every saint, sinner, and pilgrim on the inner journey as a part of God's somewhat mysterious plan. So, if we rest in God's love, perhaps we can have more humility in consolation and courage during desolate times.

✑ *A Simple Ignatian Examen* ✑

A way of testing whether our love of self is God-centered or self-centered is to ask of our moods and inner feelings when we review our day, "On whose behalf was I happy, sad, indignant, angry, delighted and so on, and who is benefiting from what I am doing?"
— Gerald Hughes, *Seven Weeks for the Soul*

There is a hunger in our hearts today to understand our lives. There is a desire in many Christians of all traditions to go more deeply within, to discern the pattern of our days with the help of the Holy Spirit. St. Ignatius of Loyola offered one way of viewing our lives from a contemplative stance, almost five hundred years ago. It is called the Examen (an examination of conscience), and it is a direct and simple way to look inward more and more, meeting the God who waits for us there. This practice has been translated through modern writers now, and so I can offer you a simple and fulfilling way to end your day and prepare your soul and heart for the day to come.

As you settle in to retire, ask yourself five questions:

1. *When was I most loving today?*

2. *When did God feel closest today?*

3. *When was I least loving today?*

4. *When did God feel farthest away?*

5. *What do I feel most grateful for this evening?*

Obviously, the answers to these questions will overlap: one will probably be coupled with two and three with four and so on. The questions exist just to spur our memories of the day and open our spirits.

Reflection upon these questions at the end of your day will inform your heart. You may rejoice in your day; you may discover things you would have handled differently had you been more aware at the moment, more willing to ask God's help. Areas of healthy self-love might be contrasted against acts of selfishness or arrogance. This should be done always keeping in mind God's unconditional love and abundant forgiveness. As Fr. Richard Rohr says in Everything Belongs, *"I believe that we have no real access to who we really are except in God. Only when we rest in God can we find the safety, the spaciousness, and the scary freedom to be who we are, all that we are, more than we are and less than we are."*

End your Examen with a simple prayer of thanksgiving:

God, I praise you for the gifts of this day, now ending.
Forgive my failings.
Keep me safe in your love as I sleep,
And help me to show love to others,
During the day to come. Amen.

Where Are You, God?

The bustle in a house
The morning after death
Is solemnest of industries
Enacted upon earth —

The sweeping up the heart,
And putting love away
We shall not want to use again
Until eternity.

> —Emily Dickinson,
> *The Selected Poems*
> *of Emily Dickinson*

Jesus wept.
—John 11:35 NRSV

LHD I was riding in the truck with my husband when his cell phone rang. It was our son, Jacques. "Dusty's dead," he said. "The oil rig he was working on in Butte LaRose blew up! He's dead."

Hot bitter tears were forced out from a place deep inside me. I cried ferociously, as confused and hurt as my son, who had just lost his best friend.

Dusty. I struggle to write about his young life. Sometimes he seemed lost and confused to me, without direction, sometimes angry. Yet, he was a country boy, simple of desire and actions. And he had a good heart, the kind that takes care of drunks and young puppies. He and Jacques built a baseball field at our house, driving posts and hauling sand. He was such a loyal friend; he had reason to treasure friendships. Once I gave Dusty a Christmas present: a gift-wrapped fleece pullover. "Gosh, Miss Lyn," he said, turning the package over in his hands, "I don't know when I last got a wrapped-up present."

Thinking of all this as I rode in the truck, I asked myself, Why didn't I do more for him? A bitter memory came to mind of my little family of three sitting snugly around the table eating three pork chops while Dusty worked outside on the baseball field. Why hadn't I persuaded him to join us? I could have cut the pork chops up. Oh, mercy, it seemed unforgivable now.

My sadness and regret deepened as we gathered at the funeral home. Jacques was experiencing his first deep grief, the first terrible situation that was totally out of his control. His eyes were those of a hunted deer as he struggled to stay one step ahead of his tears. Every time I approached him he waved me angrily away, "Not now, Mom!"

He and his other friends gathered and held each other. They were young; they would recover and go on. But Dusty wouldn't have that chance. This was the knowledge that tore at all of us.

It was only three days, but it seemed like a week before all the formalities ended and we finally parted at the cemetery. Afterward I sat in a rocker on my front porch, totally spent, deeply sad and exhausted. I was completely emptied out, without plan or bright idea. I loved Dusty, but the subtext of my grief was that tall, handsome young sons could be stripped away from their parents. Would I want to live if this happened to me? I didn't think I would.

As I rocked, a sweet desire swept over me to leave this earth, this vale of tears. God, I asked, why did you leave us here? Why must we struggle and hurt so much? Why do people come into our lives only to leave us? I want to go home! Why don't you take us home where we can all be safe and together forever... without fear?

Time passed, the dusk deepened, and my only answer came in a cool breeze against my heated face and the soft call of the mourning doves in the milo field. I wondered if Jesus wept with me. My heart eventually stilled into a sort of surrender. I knew that we would all just go on, as people had for so many centuries; we would walk into the mystery without any clear answers.

In my son's apartment are at least five pictures of Dusty: his cap stuck jauntily on his head, a cigarette between his fingers, Dusty smiling a toothy grin, looking past the camera at something else far away. Near Jacques' thermostat is the laminated obituary, stuck to the wall with a bright blue push-pin.

Dusty will always be part of Jacques and of me. I wonder now, what did I know about him? He was in so many ways a stranger, lost in the darkened corners of my life, just beyond my sight. I wish I had talked to him more, tried to understand him better. I know that his effect on my life will not end, for if I ever hesitate to offer kindness to another, I will remember Dusty and be grateful for the confused and painful love I still feel for him. It matters a lot, because I believe that the kingdom of God consists of this: that we freely offer our compassion to the stranger, even when that stranger is one of our best friends. —L.H.D.

You Have Done Great Things for Me

And blessed is she who believed that there would be a fulfillment of what was spoken to her by the Lord. —Luke 1:45 NRSV

Mary had the courage to trust in the God of the impossible and to leave the solution of her problems to him. Hers was pure faith.
—Carlo Carretto, *Blessed Are You Who Believed*

RH   I will always remember with fondness my first annunciation, the day my own angel announced to me the good news as the angel Gabriel had announced to Mary. My husband and I were having trouble conceiving a child, and my doctor confirmed on my annual visit that he was questioning whether or not I was ovulating. We scheduled an appointment three months later in August with the consideration that I might have to start on fertility drugs. I had been convinced for many years that I would never conceive, and that fearful hunch was appearing to become a reality.

That summer, as I started graduate school and was busy with nine demanding class hours, I almost forgot about my condition. Breasts swollen and a little late for my cycle, I showed up for my August appointment, a little suspicious, but not wanting to get my hopes up. Dr. Chesson advised me to drop off a urine sample the next morning. I could hardly sleep that night!

Back in 1977 there were no at-home pregnancy tests. It was actually fun having to await the results. On the morning I dropped off the specimen, I went on to class, but instead of paying attention to the exam review, I was noting my pounding heart and sweaty palms. Hands shaking, I journaled in my yellow class notebook to try to calm my spirit, scribbling: "I've prayed for serenity, I've prayed for the best outcome. I've prayed that I could prove to be the best mother possible, if he thus chooses me for that role." From the deepest place within that held my earnest desire I prayed, God, help me accept the things that I cannot change.

Watching the clock vigilantly, I left class early to phone the doctor's office. I can still hear nurse Robie's joyful declaration, "I have good news for you! Yes, honey, you are pregnant!" She could have easily said, "Hail, favored one! The Lord is with you!"

That first little baby I was so thrilled to conceive was a wonderful daughter we named Megan, who grew up to be a very strong child, often stronger than me. Divorce affected Megan differently than the other kids. My daughter and I struggled often in our relationship, and I never quit praying for new life between us.

We made it through some tough years, but something shifted when she became a mother. In fact, we became best of friends and soul companions for her mothering journey. It's like we had finally found a container for our love, helping us come to an understanding and acceptance of one another. On her first Mother's Day only weeks after the birth of her first child, Hayes, I received a card from her that is taped securely in my journal. It is one of those treasures I will save forever.

In the card she expressed how she had begun thinking since the birth of Hayes about what it means to be a mother and how to be a good one, adding that she'd read all the books so she would know how. Reading her thoughts, I had smiled to myself thinking how I, too, had thought the information gathered from books would secure for me the recognition of "Mother of the Year." Megan's honest heartfelt words that followed made up for every cross remark we had ever shared and revealed a deeper wisdom that she possessed long before I had: "And this morning (at around 3 a.m.!) when I was nursing Hayes — he started crying for no reason. And I couldn't get him to stop. So I started crying. I was overwhelmed by this tiny being, and I didn't know how to fix it. I wanted so badly to take his pain away, I would've nearly done anything. When he finally stopped, and when I finally got him to bed, I lay down to go to sleep. And I guess I couldn't fall asleep right away because my adrenaline was flowing — and I started thinking about how much I love that tiny being. And I wondered how you did this four times. And then it hit me — *you love me as much as I love him.*"

She went on to express the incredible feeling of knowing that one single person feels the same way she feels about her son — but that person feels it about her!

She concluded, "Thank you! Thank you for loving me enough to sit up and cry with me too. Because I now understand how much love it takes. I love you, Meg."

ABOUT A YEAR AGO when that little one she'd sat up with, Hayes, was just one year old, Megan announced she was pregnant again. This was not a surprise. Her little family had settled into a new home, and I knew that plans were set to have another child. I was delighted for them and excited to think of having another baby in our growing family. I'd forgotten about Megan's scheduled ultrasound until she showed up at my office door one morning, handing me the treasured photograph and bursting into joy-filled tears. As I studied the small black and white photo held in my hands, I literally tried to make a distinction between head and toe. Megan could hardly contain her bliss when she blurted out, "Mom, it's twins! I'm having twins!" We both burst into tears, doubling over in laughter. Glancing back at the picture, sure enough, I could make out two little heads, two tiny spinal cords, two teeny fetuses sharing the same womb and the same hearts of a mother and grandmother.

Megan's arrival on my doorstep that morning was a blessed visitation. Like Elizabeth and Mary, we were two women of two different generations touched by wonder and each other's love. The power of love that brings good out of brokenness continues to take my breath away, strengthening my faith in the same God who blessed Mary on that glorious day in Galilee. I know now as it was declared that day that "nothing will be impossible for God," whether that "nothing" be reconciliations, answers to fervent prayers, or two tiny babies who will face their new world side by side, cradled by a Love that never fails.   —R.H.

You Redeemed My Life

Woman, standing on a hillside, peering,
Peering into blue space.
What will woman be?
Not yet fully seen.
Not yet fully revealed,
But coming.
Coming.
— Judith Duerk, *Circle of Stones*

LHD In 1995 Jacques graduated from high school, an event weighted by greater significance for me, since he was my only child and all the other children I had longed for had never been added to our family. With his graduation a page had turned, a song of hope had finished. My grief, a muted background melody for much of Jacques' high-school career, was deep.

Knowing that I was facing the final emotional hurdles of this transition, I had scheduled an eight-day retreat on the parables of Jesus, given by well-known Jesuit priest Francis Vanderwall. But my sadness had come with me, trying to prevent my moving forward, like a huge wad of gum stuck on the bottom of my shoe. I arrived at St. Charles College on a day late in May to find that, not only did I face eight days of silence, but I was one of only two lay people there. Faced with all these factors, the familiar vinegary smell of the old buildings and the sweet grace of the sheltering oaks failed to comfort me. I was overwhelmed and ambivalent. I put on my most dangling earrings and lined my eyes with kohl. Neither priest or nun, I was determined not to be mistaken for either. I continued to struggle sadly with identity issues as the retreat progressed, and soon enough I had cried all my eye makeup away.

Who was I really? What was I to do now? What did my life mean? Why had I so lost my focus when there were abundant blessings in my life? Such very basic and deeply rooted questions moved through me like fog misting the Atchafalaya Swamp nearby. Often, spiritual answers come in particularly unexpected ways, and during this retreat they came in a dream. I was interested in dreams since they always seemed to beckon toward a rich and unrealized world within me. I had read a few books on the subject, but I had often gone for months or years without paying attention to my dreams at all.

However, on my third night at the retreat center, I had a deeply luminous dream that demanded my attention. I awoke knowing that it was significant and had been given to me as a gift to help me at this time in my life.

I am in a church and walking up the aisle to receive Communion. As I approach the altar, I gasp in surprise. There is no priest present there, but a wise old woman. Her hair is like the moss on the live oaks, her face weathered like their bark. Her hopsacking cloak covers her head and drapes around her. Her dark blue eyes are laughing, deeply knowing, mysterious. And she holds out to me, not a Communion wafer, but four brilliantly blue-green eggs. Their color was otherworldly, beautiful, and I saw that the eggs were actually pulsing with life. I turned away fearfully saying, "I'm not eating that!"

START

I was able to see Fr. Vanderwall the next day and speak to him about my dream. "Just think, Francis," I said, disturbed. "I turned away, and I rejected what was obviously the gift of the wise woman, new life being held in those eggs."

He reassured me: "Ah, you weren't ready to eat them. You would have killed them. The new life is still there, just waiting. The wise woman is there, within you, ready still to bring you new life, sacred life."

As the retreat progressed, Francis and I continued to unpack this dream daily in private sessions. He suggested some things that I could do to understand it more deeply. By treating my dream with reverence, he led me to look at all the areas of my life that were crying out for change. "What are the signs of life?" he said more than once in his rich, somewhat Indian accent, looking at me intently with his penetrating brown eyes.

And as I quietly allowed my dream to fill me with all its signs of life, the retreat silence that I had so dreaded became another gift. Sitting on a bench in the big green pasture surrounding St. Charles College, I sketched the dream, I wrote poems about it. I began to dialogue with the wise old woman in my imagination until I found out some things about her.

She was a part of me that was not concerned about what other people thought or what the rules were. She was concerned about the growth of my spirit and about the business of uncovering deep, long-denied desires, for this was where new life lay. She felt that I had important tasks still to do upon this earth and my deep desires could show me the way, and so she wanted me to write. Yes, in my heart she told me that I must overcome my fears. I must write. My grief did not magically go away, but it began to soften. Hope walked up and held my hand.

As I record this today, almost ten years later, I ask, How much do we dare believe that God is ordering our steps, opening the way we should walk? I was blessed with one of the most important dreams of my life at a time of deepest need, at the very time when Francis could escort me to the heart of its message. He guided me in letting this dream inform my life as I began to take baby steps toward a new call. This call has unfolded in gracious ways that I never thought possible.

I ponder these gifts of grace today and thank the dear wise woman that still lives within me. Perhaps she is Sophia, Lady Wisdom, another face of the life-giving God. Today, I see so many signs of life. I live in another springtime, and the swamp spiderwort blooms Madonna-blue this morning, freely offering her star-shaped flowers to the sun. Fragrant pink sage has come back for the tenth season and continues to reseed and spread beside my cottage office window. Each bit of creation gives thanks this day just through being what it is. And I give thanks through what I have been called to be: I give thanks when I call myself "writer."   —L.H.D.

Your Love
Has Changed Me

As the Father has loved me, so I have loved you; abide in my love.
— John 15:9 NRSV

God indwells us, gifts us with the Spirit, and manifests love to the world in and through us. When we live in this climate, we become, as John of the Cross phrased it, "God by participation."
— Janet Ruffing, *Spiritual Direction*

Occasionally I will read words from a spiritual text that offer the light of a new insight, like the sun suddenly breaking through on a cloudy day. Maureen Conroy's words in *Experiencing God's Tremendous Love* did just that for me several months back: "Our God — a living Person, sharing in relationship, actively present, and living Self — chooses to be affected by us. If we really believe that we make a difference to God, that our Creator would not be the same without us, that we count before God, that we can 'touch' God, then our God-as-experienced cannot be the Unmoved Mover of classical philosophy and theology. Our living God cannot be untouchable. Our loving God cannot be unaffected."

Reading her stirring words almost felt sacrilegious to my Baltimore Catechism–trained Catholic mentality. *The God of my childhood was masculine, aloof, and distant* echoed in my psyche

154

like a reprimand. But questions emerged from a consciousness that was ready to stretch and yield.

What if the God who had always seemed so distant, un-affected by me and judgmental, wanted to offer love from an intensely vulnerable stance? Could I accept that much love and consider myself worthy of it? Could I be comfortable with a God who weeps and laughs and cares so deeply about me? Would it somehow be safer to keep God so far away most of the time?

God seemed to have been setting the stage for a fundamental change in our relationship for some time. Years before, Fr. Hampton had introduced me to the notion that God desired me. Through my profound years of spiritual direction with Fr. Hampton I had begun to think of God as lover, desiring to consummate our relationship. Centering prayer had become the vehicle I used to truly experience God's love. But the corresponding thought, that God's heart could break open with love for me, that God would choose to be affected by me and my love for him, was a radically new idea, altogether exhilarating, confusing, and a bit scary. The appeal, however, was in the reciprocal nature of that blessed connection.

Reflecting further, I began to place my relationship with God as a template over my human relationships, including my marriage. I saw that these relationships, too, lacked the mutuality I was feeling called to seek with God. I desired to learn to be with another without losing myself. I wanted to love without pos-sessing, without the fear of the effects of mutual or individual growth. I longed to know that I am desirable and that another would wish to be affected by me as a result of our relationship. I pondered the thought, If God's love can change me, surely that same love can change my world.

On a recent lonely Monday morning, my relationship with God was transformed by a deeply compelling prayer experience. Before daybreak the previous day, I had bid a gloomy farewell to my husband, Easton, and twelve other missionaries leaving for the annual mission trip to Mexico that Easton and I had always co-led. But this year, God had made it clear that my mission was at home. Megan's twins were not due for five weeks, but she had given birth the preceding Thursday. The babies, although not in obvious danger, were sent to the neonatal intensive care unit. Megan was distraught and still suffering from the toxemia that had brought on the premature delivery. Her ankles looked like footballs. I felt blessed to be there to offer emotional support and physical comfort through this trying time.

I'd spent Sunday at the hospital and truly wasn't needed up there that Monday. Besides, I wanted to give her little family some time and space for bonding. Missing Easton, I wished that I could wiggle my nose to spend the day in Mexico and then come back in time to return to Lafayette General Medical Center for my night on duty. I took my suffering heart to my prayer chair.

Resting for a moment, I felt a stirring to read from Janet Ruffing's *Spiritual Direction: Beyond the Beginnings* and I began to pray with the words from a Dutch mystic, Hadewijch, quoted in the book: "For above all the gifts that I ever longed for, I chose this gift: that I should give satisfaction in all great sufferings. For that is the most perfect satisfaction: to grow up in order to be God with God."

I placed the book down and entered a contemplative silence, pondering for a moment what it might mean to grow up in order to be God with God. In stillness I waited, trusting in the Presence I was becoming accustomed to acknowledging. Graciously, God's love gradually filled my entire being, and I experienced what I have come to call boundaryless bonding, feeling God share in my sadness and isolation. God was right there suffering with me, penetrating my darkness with piercing light. He couldn't bear my being alone. I could feel something changing inside as I spoke intimately, "Jesus, I want to spend this week with you." He replied, "And me with you," moved by my need for companionship, and wanting to offer his very heart to accompany my own. I wept with acceptance.

It suddenly dawned on me that the profound Oneness with God that I had experienced occasionally on retreat and in prayer was becoming stable and consistent. Touched by an awareness of God's continuous interior presence, I was grateful that God's heart, too, might expand with my love. Returning to the hospital that afternoon, I brought with me a deep loving presence in the interior of my heart, such that my week of caretaking proved one of the most peaceful and loving ever. Jesus and I were in a redemptive partnership.

In reflecting recently on all that has happened since then, I was struck by a powerful thought. Could it be possible that the very love carried through me to my daughter throughout her ordeal in the hospital is the same love she has so patiently and generously shared with her family these last few months? As I have watched her caring for twin newborns and a two-year-old toddler, I have sensed a grace-filled peace that permeates her household. I've never felt anything like it. Did the love of God that changed me in fact change her too as it was received and shared?

Today I can honestly proclaim that the uninvolved God of my childhood is nowhere to be found. An experience of mutuality is now becoming a part of my marriage, my friendships, my mothering, and indeed most of my daily interactions with God. I no longer look to him for an answer to a plea, "Please bring my family back together!" Or a cure of my sufferings, "Please let Megan's babies be born on time so I can also serve you as a missionary!" Instead, he has become my confidant, walking with me, bringing a sacred presence to my life and offering his very heart to love with. His ever-changing, tenderly affectionate Presence permeates my being with great peace, joy, and love, even — especially — during tough and lonely times.   — R.H.

Called Forth by
Your Love

Communal spirituality brings relationship with other human beings to the fore.... Our culture is becoming more and more aware that life is a community affair, that salvation is a community experience, and that building the realm of God here on earth is a community endeavor. —John English, *Spiritual Freedom*

LHD I have an ongoing joke with two beloved fellow music ministers: Linda Vollmer and Linda Bergeron. When the three of us work together, we are two Lindas and a Lyn. Couple this with the fact that Linda Bergeron calls Linda Vollmer "Lynn" and you have an interesting recipe for miscommunication, sometimes rising to the pitch of *Who's on First?*

On a recent Wednesday evening, the two Lindas and I were presenting an original play centered on the Samaritan woman at the well in John's Gospel. I had written the short play and the song that accompanied it. Linda Vollmer was to act the part of the Samaritan woman, and Linda Bergeron was to play Jesus.

At around six, those participating in the Rite of Christian Initiation for Adults, persons who wish to become members of the Catholic Church, began to arrive through my front door. There was Martha, a pretty woman with dark eyes and hair, newly arrived from Texas. She was accompanied by her two lovely teenage daughters and one gentle, polite teenage son.

There was a shy man in his late twenties and another woman dressed in jeans who smiled kindly at me as she entered my home. To round out the group was a striking lady, Jean, in her late fifties, dressed in a lovely turquoise silk suit and groomed to perfection.

Now Linda Vollmer placed a purple drape over her head and walked into the space that we had decorated with a small, working fountain, several rocks, and a green plant or two. I began to play and sing:

> If only you knew. . . .
> If only you knew. . . .
> This water I'm offering you.
> Is source and spirit, life and dream.
> The mystic water of Jesus . . . the Lord.
>
> She came to the well all alone,
> Sad and weary, in pain.
> Every road
> She had taken . . .
> Wound back to the same place . . .
> Again.

Linda Bergeron, as Jesus, stood and greeted the woman in purple and began to speak to her. My living room was transformed to a dry, dusty place beside a well that existed two thousand years ago, scene of the legendary encounter between a lost and thirsty woman and the man who came to bring living water. As the dialogue paused, I sang,

> She chided the man at the well,
> Saying you have no bucket, no cord.

With love, he observed her.
And gave the hope, she'd never had
Before.

Never thirst again!
Be no longer poor!

As I played the appropriate chords on the piano, I was struck by the beautiful ways our gifts come together to serve others. God's touch in my life has not been just for me but for community. Author Gerald Collins says this of finding ourselves wiser at midlife: "This new wisdom involves self-discovery, but not self-seeking. Those who have found a new center and an integrating factor have now a confident message to deliver. They demonstrate the paradox of a movement towards themselves which has brought them back to others. . . . Fresh responsibilities begin. For the benefit of others they live out what they have experienced for themselves" (*The Second Journey: Spiritual Awareness and the Mid-Life Crisis*).

Our coming home to ourselves and our gifts is for service in the world. Tiny Linda Vollmer with her white hair is a tireless worker, directing three choirs and bringing music to countless liturgies. She visits nursing homes and homebound people with her children's choir to bring a little joy to the elderly and infirm. She is always ready to try the new thing, like this play.

Linda Bergeron is my age, a mother of five and grandmother, a psychotherapist and artist who suffered through the deaths of her mother and her younger sister in one year. She encountered many physical problems as stress took its toll. Yet her skill in design shone forth in my home that evening, as a few stones and some swirled fabric became the place where Grace spoke its truth.

As I viewed the pretty tableau in my living room my mind drifted back over the almost thirty years that I have participated in music ministry, in part because of the encouragement of both of these women. I have now sung at numerous funerals, praying deeply within my heart that I could bring some comfort to the grieving. I have been able to put my own fear of death aside for a moment, as I looked at yet another pall-draped coffin and prayed that my death would be peaceful and my own passing filled with love, joy, and beautiful song.

We have sung at First Communions, where the bright eyes of small boys and girls filled us with hope. Dressed in their finest, they were celebrated by their parents, friends, and relatives on their special day. They were told of their worth and showered with love. Let love fill them, I have prayed. Let them always know that they are loved and worthy of love.

There have been bad days. Practices at night when everyone was tired and irritable from a day's work and other times when no one came to practice and I had to ditch that beautiful new song we were going to learn that exactly fit the readings of the day. I remembered those Masses in the past when the guitarist had the capo on the wrong fret and didn't match the piano and everything dissolved into chaos, when my voice broke, my fingers froze over the F sharp minor with an A in the bass and half the choir came in at the wrong time and I went home and told Dee, "I'm quitting." But I didn't.

And because it is all about service and not perfection, it seems a miracle of grace when the entire choir is there and Lisa's fabulous contralto voice harmonizes with Cody's clear soaring tenor and Benny picks a C-major seventh chord with his magic fingers on the guitar. I look into the congregation and see a dear elderly lady wiping a tear and smiling softly at the same time and you can just take me to heaven right then. In fact sometimes I believe I have arrived.

Anyone involved in the work of church knows that there are occasional resentments and miscommunications as well as loving rapport and joy. Recently I have been coping with my anger at the institutional church and its policies, especially concerning women, and I don't know where my future is leading. Love is nothing if not demanding, and answers must be found within each person. I would like to say that prayer solves it all, but as many of us know, service in a church community must be lived daily. As I grow in faith, the boundaries of my community broaden and deepen, encompassing so much more, so many more. Perhaps this too is the fruit of prayer.

Now on this special evening in my home, the play in my living room ended as the Samaritan woman turned to announce, "Come and see the man who told me everything, the man who understands me and loves me. The man who forgives! He is the messiah."

He is the messiah, the one who sees over the next hill when I don't. God is with me here and now as I live out my gifts in brokenness and joy, anger, weariness, and beauty. I think our service can only come from our response to the life of God within us. We are then growing streams of living water, fed from a boundless source.   —L.H.D.

When Women Pray

When you meet someone at the level of prayer, you meet them on the ground of eternity. This is the heart of all kinship and affinity.
— John O'Donohue, *Eternal Echoes*

For where two or three are gathered in my name, I am there among them. — Matthew 18:20 NRSV

RH It was a Saturday morning, a blessed day of Sabbath, perched right in the middle of a few very hectic weeks. I was drawn to stay home for a quiet morning with Easton, but I knew myself too well. I would poison the shared solitude with work on the series of Advent talks I was preparing for an upcoming parish mission, workaholic that I can be. So I chose instead to do what my soul had committed to weeks before, participate in my first labyrinth walk. I took off for St. Mary's Catholic Church, only a block from my home, and used the brief strolling time to pray for the grace to let go, to surrender to the present moment, to release once again my control of time, my schedule, my to-do list. Turning the corner and glimpsing the image of the spiraling sun on the stained-glass doors of the parish hall, I sensed the engagement in my soul. I needed this day of Sabbath. I thanked God for calling me here.

Joining with about thirty other Theresians from various communities all over the city, we gathered together in preparation for Advent. I was a bit reticent, yet reassured by the fact that it was no accident that I would walk my first labyrinth with some of the women with whom I had journeyed more than twenty years. Among the community of seekers were those who have challenged me to grow and pray, to stretch and listen and serve, to become the woman God calls me to be.

Sitting in a darkened classroom listening to the introductory remarks of the facilitator, my heart softened. "I am a woman within a community within a community within a community." I was surrounded by the enduring love of so many women, comforted by the resonating thought *I belong.* Through the years, God has created within me a blessed sense of belonging: amid Theresian sisters, loyal friends and chosen prayer partners, as well as the women of my family and lineage — daughters, sisters, mother, grandmothers, and aunts. I have always referred to the precious women of my life as my "communion of saints." We, seekers and pilgrims, share the same yearning in our souls, all desiring God through prayer.

My mind floated to another space and time, as I reflected on the rich spiritual heritage to which I have always belonged. I was flooded with memories of being privy to another's prayers. I saw myself as an adolescent, peering at Aunt Mickey kneeling by her bed, elbows draped forward. I sensed her desire. I imagined she was seeking God's grace to help her raise her five children. Her husband had died when the little one was three days old. Sometimes in her praying, she cried. I must have absorbed her faith, her love of God, her seeking heart, even some of her pain.

I could hear my grandmother, Mon Mon (pronounced "Maw Maw"), praying the Rosary with Pa Pa from behind the closed door of their bedroom in our home, the room they assumed after my brother went to college. I appreciated recalling the faithful sounds of the Hail Marys I'd overheard so many years ago much more that day than I had as a teenager. Back then, when they were living with us, it was an invasion, though I drew comfort even as a teen that I was one of the ten children and forty-two grandchildren whose needs they carried in their hearts and on those beads. I felt grateful that their prayers and faith unquestionably helped to form my own.

My mind lingered in the past, as suddenly I could smell the incense and view the shiny terrazzo floors of St. Dominic's Church. I was sitting in a pew beside Mamma, listening to her sobs the weeks following Daddy's death, silently sharing her prayers of grief. I must have sensed that in those difficult days, her only consolation was God. I have drawn time and time again on that same reassurance.

Glancing once again at my contemporaries sitting in the classroom beside me, I felt blessed and comforted by their presence. We moved to the parish hall, where I got my first real view of the canvas labyrinth sprawled from wall to wall across the floor. It was mesmerizing to behold. Purple-painted scallops bordered the circular pattern. It looked like a maze, but I've been told it's not. A maze is dead-ended, but the labyrinth is a walking prayer path that takes you to the center via a meandering pathway, and then out again. Symbolically it represents the journey to the center of the self, to the heart of God.

I glanced around at the prayerful environment assembled with love; lighted candles, colorful scarves, beautiful feminine art, and sacred music filled the room. I was eager to embark on my journey in the silent contemplative space shared with my sisters. I entered the labyrinth expectantly and immediately began to absorb the love emanating from the heart of each woman present. I was strengthened at once by the silent recognition that our journeys, though each extraordinarily different, are elementally the same.

The first pilgrim I noticed was Fern, her white hair tucked beneath a blue veil. She was walking slowly, bowed and serious. I smiled inside, moved that this elderly woman was choosing to share in the experience that morning. I wondered about her life and what her concerns were. She appeared lonely to me. I was glad she was there with us.

For a few moments, I walked alongside Bonnie, who had endured a painful divorce many years ago, about the same time I had. As we passed each other on the path, our hearts locked in an unvoiced acknowledgment of mutual hurts from the past, and yet, with an appreciation of the kindred joy inherent in our resurrected lives. Georgie, Ann, and Carolyn paused to offer a hug. Their love was palpable.

Claire observed my tears and gently placed her hands on my shoulders to lead me around the labyrinth. I was touched by an awareness that after years of my guiding Claire in workshop settings and retreats, the roles were powerfully reversed that morning. I surrendered to her direction and experienced the vulnerability of being steered across the labyrinth and outside the designated path. I paid attention to the discomfort with the recognition that my spirituality has so often been linear and restricted by my self-inflicted need to please and follow the rules. As I walked across the sacred spiral path, I felt free and utterly content.

My moist eyes beheld Gloria and Margie. Gloria's hands rested firmly on Margie's shoulders. Both wept as they carefully strolled across the path in tandem. The naked trust of those two remarkable women drew a desire for such faith in my own soul. Gloria is blind. I wanted to trust another so completely.

After about an hour, I exited the labyrinth almost sad to leave, though certainly filled and deeply reflective. Sitting in silence to process my experience, I was flooded with thankfulness for that grace-filled event and the countless other times I have had the privilege of sharing in community with other women.

IT DAWNED ON ME that there *is* something special when women pray, something unseen, unspoken, but very, very real, that binds us all. We become company for each other in our discovery of God as if we walk the same labyrinth with those who pray with us, those whom we know and those we have never met. We access a love that stretches back over the years — to the women of the Old Testament, Mary the mother of Jesus, and the blessed unnamed woman at the well. It's the same love that transcends culture, like that of the women I gather with in Mexico. The only language we share is love, a love that binds us in a profound oneness and a knowing that we women all share the same concerns no matter where we live. This love reaches toward the mystery of the future, as women's lives change and we struggle with trying to do, be, and have it all, only to find that the meaning may be in the struggle and not in the *having* at all. It is a love even great enough to cradle the abused, the oppressed, and the discounted all over the world.

What happens when women pray? They find the God within and without. This tender God of love calls them down paths they never thought they could tread, yet he's also a demanding God. Growth and service are not options but commands for women who pray. God calls us forth to use our gifts and talents, and even our struggles as we bring forth new life in the world. I couldn't help but imagine that when women come together to pray, heaven must rejoice in our vulnerability, strength, wisdom, and love.

FILLED WITH THESE THOUGHTS, I returned home with a profound fullness and gratitude brought on by that sacred experience. I thanked God again for the blessing of my sisters. The blessings of us all, when women pray.   —R.H.

Epilogue

RH On a recent Monday morning, I awakened with a chuckle. I had just been called "ovulatory" by my boss and pastor, Fr. Chester, in an early morning dream.

"Ovulatory?" I exclaimed! "What does *that* mean?"

"You know... ovulatory. Intense. Robin, you're just too serious at times. You need to lighten up," he explained light-heartedly.

Upon awakening, I immediately shared my secret word with Easton. I just couldn't trust my forgetful mind with such a gem.

As the week progressed, I noticed the accused intensity literally under my skin. I noted hints of a familiar female condition, the dreaded PMS, only this time it seemed to persist throughout the week. As my symptoms lingered, I couldn't help but wonder if these were a warning sign of menopause. I pondered how forgetful I'd become and how it was beginning to scare me. Was the dream perhaps an announcement?

By Thursday, I was at my Theresian meeting. Always captivated by my love of these women, that morning I was viewing our sacred space through a different lens — my own orneriness. During our leadership discernment process, an annual ritual that I have led for our community so many times over our twenty years of monthly gatherings, I noticed one of our members forget whom she had called forth to serve on the previous round. We're really aging, I thought to myself. I was caught off guard when another member gave unsolicited advice to me to stop manipulating the process. My need to control was oozing out from under my skin. When the meeting ended, I was not feeling really good about myself. Later on that day, Lyn called me "strong." It wasn't meant to be a compliment. Was I on the road to becoming a crotchety old lady?

God seemed to have a say about all this that same afternoon. In a grace-filled moment while praying *lectio divina* with the group of female college students I gather with weekly, there was no doubt as to the invitation being delivered. A line in the Gospel of John stirred in my heart, and I felt like I was standing on a precipice glancing fearfully at the next stage of my life. Peter had just been asked three times by Jesus if the apostle loved him. Jesus responded to Peter's affirmations with the command "Then tend and feed my sheep." The very next line seemed to lift off the page, demanding my attention: "Amen, amen I say to you, when you were younger you used to dress yourself and go where you wanted; when you grow old, you will stretch out your hands, and someone else will dress you and lead you where you do not want to go" (John 21:18).

As I discussed the connected events of the week in spiritual direction on Friday, Sr. Gloria asked a stirring question: "Robin, are you comfortable with change?" She seemed to be signaling a curve ahead in my journey's path. I can't say I liked the question, but from deep inside there was a *knowing* that I was indeed changing, that I was entering another phase of my life, with the invitation to stretch out my hands and allow Another to lead me where I might not necessarily like to go. Yuk.

As I considered what change might lie ahead, I felt flustered. Hadn't I finally arrived in a much-deserved place of consolation?

After seemingly eons of heartaches and kid-raising, couldn't I take it easy, at least for a while? I really had been living in what seemed like a bubble of grace for the past few years, and I didn't want it to burst.

I chuckled to myself as I realized how I have viewed change.

Driving home yesterday, while listening to a CD from a conference Paula D'Arcy had recently led with Richard Rohr, I reconsidered the concept. To me, Paula has embraced the invitation to change as a holy calling, sacramentally entering and reentering change throughout a life that's borne incredible fruits. These profound recorded words spoken by both Richard and Paula washed over me and penetrated my spirit with a summons: *Let go.*

"Grace always changes you. . . .

"We would rather have stability over grace. . . .

"What will become of me if I completely surrender to God's grace? What will become of me if I do not? . . .

"God is demanding my whole heart: 'If you give me half your heart, I will give you half my power. If you give me all your heart, I will change your life.' "

I heard Paula's words inside of myself: "Something is being demanded of me at this juncture. . . . "

In preparing my soul for this *change of life,* I prayerfully respond to Jesus, "Yes, Lord, I will tend your sheep. I extend my arms and allow you to lead me, perhaps where I don't want to go. I offer you my whole heart, not just half of it, and so I surrender completely to your grace. And yes, Lord, use me. You use me."

—R.H.

LHD I have been laughing about Robin's dream for days. Last night I sat down to watch the final episode of *Frasier,* and I recalled the statement "Robin, you're too ovulatory," and I started laughing until I got up, turned off the television, and just sat wiping tears of laughter away.

The obvious meaning of her dream to me is new life, a fitting theme for this epilogue. I have been pondering what is newly growing in my life. I know that I am seeing things in new ways as though scales have fallen from my eyes. I have fewer knee-jerk reactions regarding politics, religion, or personal life. Now I almost always understand both sides of any issue, and while this does not make me comfortable, perhaps it makes me wiser. My vision has grown wider and I see God everywhere, in everything and everyone. Writer Rita Winters says it this way: "It must pain God that we cannot see the world as it is, that we continue to think in simpleton fashion and divide creation into dualities." Fr. Richard Rohr describes this new way of being as "seeking the third way."

I sought the third way recently when I struggled about whether to leave music ministry to devote my time fully to writing and spiritual direction. When I asked myself, Do I leave or do I stay? my inner voice said, "Seek a third way." Richard Rohr describes this as resisting a simple fight or flight response, holding on to our position between attachment and detachment. He says that we must hold the pain until it transforms us. When I resisted a flight or attach decision, I came up with the idea of sharing responsibility with others in my choir and deciding on a month-by-month basis whether I can be present at particular practices or liturgies. This creative solution is working well, and I wouldn't have known to consider this until recently because my thinking was so black and white.

New life for me is reminding myself to listen to the inner voice of God who is always speaking, though drowned out by the noise and clutter of my life. This voice has lately given me the courage to speak back to those with power, something I have rarely, if ever, done. I recently wrote two respectful yet dissenting letters to an archbishop concerning recent events in his diocese that involved women. I was upset about his handling of these situations. I am under no illusions that my letters will bring great change, but they were something I could do and something I felt I should do. This action felt scary but it resonated as necessary if I am to leave perpetual childhood and do the work I am called to do rather than what the world clamors for me to do. My calling Robin "strong" was an obvious projection of my uneasiness with my own strength. I have been told by friends and those not so friendly for years that I am a strong woman, but I was never comfortable with that information, I guess because of cultural conditioning that made me equate this quality with being unfeminine. Because of God's love and a growth in self-acceptance I now have the courage to be strong. I seek to be strong and wise, compassionate and courageous in doing good work. With all my heart, I wish you the same strength on your sacred path as it unfolds day by day.

It is appropriate to speak of new life as spring unfolds vibrantly all around me. I have shared my love of the earth throughout this book. Increasingly I embrace this felt love as deeply meaningful in my life, looking for where it might lead me. As a beginning, I hope that my writing will help others to see what an incredible gift our earth is. I will leave you, dear readers, with a final experience of this gift.

A few nights ago, the sun had just set when I walked into the sugarcane field behind my house. It was vibrating with the life of a south Louisiana May evening; the air was misty and the trees were filled with the hidden swoosh of birds and the heavy exuberance of new leaves. Taffy, my dog, darted around at my ankles, sniffing the air. The canes stood about two feet high, and as I walked among them I thought, How did I wind up in a place of such beauty? How could I be so fortunate?

Then I saw them. The fireflies! Their tiny diamond-lights were darting up and down among the plants, filling the rows; there were hundreds of them! Zigging and zagging they danced in the rows, bringing the stars to the earth. I stood on tiptoe and lifted my arms to heaven. Then I knelt and touched the ground with deep reverence. I couldn't possibly have held another thing in my heart.

Thank you and praise you, dear and loving God. Amen.

—L.H.D.

Suggested Favorite Readings

1. Wiederkehr, Macrina, O.S.B. *A Tree Full of Angels: Seeing the Holy in the Ordinary.* San Francisco: HarperCollins, 1988. This spiritual treasure offers the reader the opportunity to enter the inner life of this Benedictine monk through her very personal encounters with God. I have read it over and over again and used it as a guide countless times in group spiritual direction.

2. Rohr, Richard. *Everything Belongs: The Gift of Contemplative Prayer.* New York: Crossroad, 1999; revised and updated edition, 2003. Richard Rohr prophetically opens the minds of those who are serious about the sacred journey to truly see life differently. Reading this book created in me nothing less than a transformation of mind and heart. I recommend it to every directee.

3. Silf, Margaret. *Inner Compass: An Invitation to Ignatian Spirituality.* Chicago: Loyola Press, 1999. A lively and highly relevant guide to the Spiritual Exercises of St. Ignatius. This book helps people pray through their days with Scripture in a timeless, yet individual way.

4. Nouwen, Henri J. M. *The Inner Voice of Love: A Journey through Anguish to Freedom.* New York: Image Doubleday Books, 1996. Every book that I have ever read by Henri Nouwen has reached that place in my soul where pain and triumph meet, the place where God longs to dwell fully, if we but invite God in. Reading this book is having the experience of

God speaking personally to me and soothing my every wound and fear.

5. Rupp, Joyce. *Dear Heart, Come Home: The Path of Midlife Spirituality.* New York: Crossroad, 1996. Joyce Rupp has the wonderful ability to make the complex journeys of our lives deeply symbolic and accessible. She takes the experience of God's love from the individual to the universal and shows us how to pray in many ways. I have prayed deeply with all of her books.

6. Duerk, Judith. *Circle of Stones: Woman's Journey to Herself.* Makawao, Maui, Hawaii: Inner Ocean, 1999. Judith Duerk created a classic in this book on the woman's inner journey. Breaking through hardened cultural consciousness she shows how things might have been — might still be — different for the souls of women. She invites women to find their woman-soul and live an authentic life. (Not specifically Christian.)

7. Cameron, Julia, and Mark Bryan. *The Artist's Way: A Spiritual Path to Higher Creativity.* New York: G. P. Putnam's Sons, 1992. At first glance, this doesn't seem to be a book about prayer, but after ten years of personal and group experiences with this text, I can assure you that it is. The authors blaze a spiritual trail, not just for creativity recovery, but for recovery of one's authentic soul. This book changed my life. (Not specifically Christian.)

8. Kidd, Sue Monk. *When the Heart Waits: Spiritual Direction for Life's Sacred Questions.* San Francisco: HarperCollins, 1992. This is a must read for every woman passing through midlife. The richness of Sue's own journey as well as sound information for spiritual seekers offer a profound combination of reading material to accompany one's journey.

9. Thibodeaux, Mark E., S.J. *Armchair Mystic: Easing into Contemplative Prayer.* Cincinnati: St. Anthony Messenger Press,

2001. A text that serves as a guide for anyone serious about prayer. It is beautifully written, yet technical and thorough in presentation, simple, yet deep.

10. Muller, Wayne. *Sabbath: Restoring the Sacred Rhythm of Rest.* New York: Bantam Books, 1999. Reading this book feels like an experience of Sabbath. It is truly life-changing, offering permission to rest, the central ingredient to a balanced, prayerful life.

11. Winters, Rita. *the Green Desert: A silent Retreat.* New York: Crossroad, 2004. Rita Winters almost gives us the treat of two books in one in *The Green Desert.* As we enjoy and learn from her time of solitude in the natural setting of an Arizona desert retreat house, we also are graced with her deep insights about all the books she treasured reading there. She provides the reader with a rich smorgasbord of choices for spiritual reading and growth. I wanted to pack a suitcase of books and retreat to the desert after I read her charming and informative account of a deeply uplifting journey.

Bibliography

Ahern, Patrick, *Maurice and Thérèse*. New York: Doubleday, 1998.

Artress, Lauren. *Walking a Sacred Path*. New York: Riverhead Books, 1996.

Au, Wilkie, S.J. *By Way of the Heart: Towards a Holistic Christian Spirituality*. New York and Mahwah, N.J.: Paulist Press, 1989.

Baab, Lynne M. *A Renewed Spirituality: Finding Fresh Paths at Midlife*. Downers Grove, Ill.: InterVarsity Press, 2002.

Baker, Carolyn Nabors. *Caught in a Higher Love: Inspiring Stories of Women in the Bible*. Nashville: Broadman and Holman, 1998.

Benner, David G. *Surrender to Love: Discovering the Heart of Christian Spirituality*. Downers Grove, Ill.: InterVarsity Press, 2003.

Cameron, Julia, and Mark Bryan. *The Artist's Way: A Spiritual Path to Higher Creativity*. New York: G. P. Putnam's Sons, 1992.

Carretto, Carlo. *Blessed Are You Who Believed*. Maryknoll, N.Y.: Orbis Books, 1983.

Cavolina, Jane, and Matthew Bunson. *All Shall Be Well: Hope and Inspiration from Great Catholic Thinkers*. New York: Berkley, 2004.

Chalon, Jean. *Thérèse of Lisieux: A Life of Love*. Liguori, Mo.: Liguori Publications, 1997.

Conroy, Maureen, R.S.M. *Experiencing God's Tremendous Love: Entering into Relational Prayer*. Mahwah, N.J.: Paulist Press, 1996.

Crosby, Cindy. *By Willoway Brook: Exploring the Landscape of Prayer*. Brewster, Mass.: Paraclete Press, 2003.

Curtis, Brent, and John Eldredge. *The Sacred Romance: Drawing Closer to the Heart of God.* Nashville: Thomas Nelson, 1997.

D'Arcy, Paula. *Gift of the Red Bird: A Spiritual Encounter.* New York: Crossroad, 1996.

————. *Seeking with All My Heart.* New York: Crossroad, 2003.

DeMeester, Conrad, O.C.D. *The Power of Confidence.* New York: Alba House, 1998.

Dickinson, Emily. *The Collected Poems of Emily Dickinson.* New York: Barnes and Noble Classics, 2003.

Dupré, Louis, and James A. Wiseman. *Light from Light: An Anthology of Christian Mysticism.* New York: Paulist Press, 2001.

Duerk, Judith. *Circle of Stones: Woman's Journey to Herself.* Makawao, Maui, Hawaii: Inner Ocean, 1999.

Eliot, T. S. *Four Quartets.* Orlando, Fla.: Harcourt, 1943.

English, John J. *Spiritual Freedom: From an Experience of the Ignatian Exercises to the Art of Spiritual Guidance.* 2nd ed. Chicago: Loyola Press, 1995.

Flanagan, Sabina. *Hildegard of Bingen: A Visionary Life.* New York: Barnes and Noble, 1990.

Fox, Matthew. *Illuminations of Hildegard of Bingen.* Rochester, Vt.: Bear and Company, 2002.

Gunn, Robert Jingen. *Journeys into Emptiness: Dogen, Merton, Jung and the Quest for Transformation.* New York and Mahwah N.J.: Paulist Press, 2000.

Hauser, Richard, S.J. *In His Spirit: A Guide to Today's Spirituality.* New York: Paulist Press, 1982.

Hughes, Gerald W. *Seven Weeks for the Soul: A Reflective Journey for Lent or Other Times of Renewal.* Chicago: Loyola Press, 2001.

Hutchinson, Gloria. *A Retreat with Gerard Manley Hopkins and Hildegard of Bingen: Turning Pain into Power.* Cincinnati: St. Anthony Messenger Press, 1995.

Keating, Thomas. *Awakenings.* New York: Crossroad, 2000.

Kidd, Sue Monk. *When the Heart Waits: Spiritual Direction for Life's Sacred Questions.* San Francisco: HarperCollins, 1992.

Kushner, Harold S. *How Good Do We Have to Be? A New Understanding of Guilt and Forgiveness.* Boston: Little, Brown, 1996.

Levine, Julia B. *Practicing for Heaven.* Tallahassee Fla.: Anhinga Press, 1999.

Maddocks, Fiona. *Hildegard of Bingen: The Woman of Her Age.* New York and London: Image Books, Doubleday, 2001.

McDonnel, Thomas P., ed. *A Thomas Merton Reader.* New York and London: Image Books, Doubleday. 1989.

Moore, Thomas. *Care of the Soul: A Guide for Cultivating Depth and Awareness in Everyday Life.* New York: HarperPerennial, 1994.

Muller, Wayne. *Sabbath: Restoring the Sacred Rhythm of Rest.* New York: Bantam Books, 1999.

Norris, Kathleen. *Amazing Grace: A Vocabulary of Faith.* New York: Riverhead Books, 1996.

———. *The Cloister Walk.* New York: Riverhead Books, 1996.

O'Collins, Gerald, *The Second Journey: Spiritual Awareness and the Mid-Life Crisis.* New York: Paulist Press, 2003.

O'Donohue, John. *Eternal Echoes.* New York: HarperCollins, 1999.

Ortlund, Anne. *Disciplines of the Beautiful Woman.* Nashville: W. Publishing Group, 1977.

Palmer, Parker. *Let Your Life Speak: Listening for the Voice of Vocation.* San Francisco: Jossey-Bass, 2000.

Rohr, Richard. *Everything Belongs: The Gift of Contemplative Prayer.* New York: Crossroad, 1999.

———. *Simplicity.* New York: Crossroad, 2003.

Ruffing, Janet K., R.S.M. *Spiritual Direction: Beyond the Beginnings.* Mahwah, N.J.: Paulist Press, 2000.

Rupp, Joyce. *The Cosmic Dance: An Invitation to Experience Our Oneness.* Maryknoll, N.Y.: Orbis Books, 2002.

———. *Dear Heart, Come Home: A Path of Midlife Spirituality.* New York: Crossroad, 1996.

Sanford, John. *Mystical Christianity: A Psychological Commentary on the Gospel of John.* New York: Crossroad, 1999.

Steindl-Rast, David. *Gratefulness, the Heart of Prayer.* New York: Paulist Press, 1984.

Thérèse of Lisieux, St. *St. Thérèse of Lisieux: General Correspondence.* Vols. 1 and 2. Trans. John Clarke. Washington, D.C.: ICS Publications, 1996.

———. *Story of a Soul: The Autobiography of St. Thérèse of Lisieux.* 3rd ed. Ed. John Clarke, O.C.D. Trans. from the original manuscripts. Washington, D.C.: ICS Publications, 1996.

Thomas à Kempis. *The Imitation of Christ.* Trans. William C. Creasy. Notre Dame, Ind.: Ave Maria Press, 1989.

Thibodeaux, Mark E., S.J. *Armchair Mystic: Easing into Contemplative Prayer.* Cincinnati: St. Anthony Messenger Press, 2001.

Tolle, Eckhart. *The Power of Now: A Guide to Spiritual Enlightenment.* Navato, Calif.: New World Library, 2003.

Voss, Elwood C., Patricia Mullen, et al. *The Theresian Story: Women in Support of Women.* Colorado Springs, Colo.: Theresian Publications, 1986.

Wiederkehr, Macrina, O.S.B. *A Tree Full of Angels: Seeing the Holy in the Ordinary.* San Francisco: HarperCollins, 1988.

———. *Behold Your Life.* Notre Dame, Ind.: Ave Maria Press, 2000.

Winters, Rita. *The Green Desert: A Silent Retreat.* New York: Crossroad, 2004.

Wolfe, Pierre, ed. The *Spiritual Exercises of St. Ignatius: A New Translation from the Authorized Latin Text.* Liguori, Mo.: Liguori/Triumph, 1997.

Acknowledgments

from Lyn

Nothing is created in isolation. As I thought of those I wanted to thank for their help in this project, so many people came to mind. First, there is my husband, Dee, whose cushioning support of my life makes it possible for me to write daily. He truly shows his love in actions every single day.

My friend Vinita Hampton Wright, author and midwife to authors, I thank for helping me in so many ways to become a better writer.

I want to thank the St. Joseph Wings Choir, especially Deacon Cody Miller for his support of this project and his unwavering service to our church flock in Milton, Louisiana. And I want to thank Fr. Keith LaBove, who has been available to answer questions for all my books and has lent his loving support to my creative endeavors.

Thanks to Darlene Broussard, who helped me greatly with the technical aspects of this book and called me to pledge her ongoing support. Her quiet competence increased my own.

Acknowledgement goes out to my writing circle: Joan, Avis, Kathleen, and Guy, who have listened to my stories and given feedback and encouragement to me. And to my Theresian sisters, who give me the hugs and the smiles I need to keep writing. To Teenie Renfro, a best friend, who gives me unconditional love and always makes me laugh and put things in perspective. To Pat Low and the staff at Crossroads Catholic Bookstore, whose tender care of my books has warmed my heart. And to Ricky and Chris Broussard, faithful, helpful friends.

To my dear directees and others who have allowed me to share bits of their sacred walk, *Thank you!*

My writing partner, Robin, has been a teacher in my life. She faces problems squarely and works things out. Her soul really is pure. Having a writing partner has been pure gold for me, a sacred alchemy. I believe that we have brought out the best in one another. I love you, Robin.

Roy M. Carlisle, senior editor at Crossroad Publishing Company, has nursed this project from a little bitty Advent book to the much richer work that it is today. I have never dug so deep or shared so much. Just knowing his expectations were high gave me the confidence to lay everything on the page.

And finally, thanks to Jacques Doucet, my son, whose presence on this earth lights up my life. How did I ever get so fortunate?

from Robin

For years I have dreamed of publishing a list of those whose paths have touched my own in a sacred way. I am deeply moved by this opportunity and pray that even those whose names aren't mentioned know in their souls my deep love of them.

Thank you,

Easton, for sharing my love of marriage, contemplative prayer, and the Catholic faith. Your support and patience throughout this project have been priceless.

Megan, Ryan, Emily, and Michael, for your love of me and each other, your humor, and your eager participation in this project, especially as I have shared so much from your own lives. Thank you for your tender hearts.

Mom, for believing in me all my life and for teaching me how to love, how to listen, and how to mother.

Archbishop Harry J. Flynn, Fr. Hampton Davis, Sr. Gloria Murillo, Fr. Don Piraro, my spiritual directors. Your wisdom and love have shaped my spiritual journey, giving me the desire to do the same for others.

Fr. Chester Arceneaux and Fr. Curtis Mallet, my pastors, for believing in me and trusting in my wisdom.

Daughters of Wisdom and the students, parishioners, and staff of Our Lady of Wisdom Catholic Church and Student Center, for sharing so intimately the spiritual journey.

My countless friends whom I wish I could name personally. There are four I must mention: Corky, Pat, Karen, and Renola. Thank you for your undying support and trust, for your loyalty and devotion to sharing the journey.

Millie, Denise, Tessa, Nikki, Stephanie, and Ellen, my prayer partners, whose prayers sustained me throughout this project.

Vicki Schmidt, executive director of Theresians of the United States, for your loving support of this project and of the journey shared in community.

Sarah Johnson. Your belief in us and kind, affirming words helped me to believe in myself as a writer. Thank you for the hours you spent offering feedback and professional expertise.

Paula D'Arcy, whose written and spoken words helped to birth my own. Thank you, Paula, for your encouragement and love, and for putting Lyn and me in touch with Roy.

Roy, our editor, for believing in us "Daughters of the South" and for assisting us to dig deeper into our experiences. Roy, you told us in the beginning that you wanted us to give of our deepest and most authentic selves in a way that would usher the reader into another door that is closer to the Holy of Holies. Thank you for drawing that out and for giving us permission to *show and tell* another about being in God's presence.

Lyn, for trusting me, for being patient and tender, wise and instructive. It is truly no accident that I would write my first book within the context of community. I can't imagine having done it with anyone else. The trust we have built is the gift of a lifetime.

About the Authors

LYN HOLLEY DOUCET is the author of *Water From Stones: An Inner Journey,* which won a Catholic Press Award in 2002. Her second book was recently released from Loyola Press in Chicago: *A Healing Walk with St. Ignatius: Finding God in Difficult Times.*

She grew up on a cotton farm in north Louisiana, with three siblings, where she developed a deep love of the natural world. She has fond memories of growing up in a loving community in her Methodist church in Bastrop. Lyn was welcomed into the Catholic Church in 1972. She is from a family that includes Methodists, Episcopalians, Baptists, and those of no organized religion. Lyn is very comfortable with diversity.

Her undergraduate degree is in Speech and English from Louisiana State University. She has a master's degree in Education from the University of Louisiana–Lafayette. After being in public school work for twenty years with special needs children, she is now a spiritual director, retreat master, and composer. She leads a liturgical ensemble at St. Joseph Church in Milton, Louisiana.

She is active at various retreat houses and for the Diocese of Lafayette. Her talks combine storytelling, biblical text, humor, and her personal witness in a highly informative and enjoyable format. Lyn directs people in prayer and Ignatian spirituality at her home in Maurice. She has also taught *Artist's Way* and Creativity courses at the University of Louisiana's leisure learning center. She is currently recording an original series of guided Gospel meditations with Louisiana composer and musician Walter Poussan Jr.

She has had a twice-monthly radio program, *Water from Stones*, on Radio Maria, the international Vatican radio station. She and her radio partner, Sharon O'Neill, have discussed a variety of subjects from women in the Bible to "the Christian midlife crisis."

She lives with her husband of thirty-one years near Maurice, Louisiana; he is a residential contractor. Their son, Jacques, is twenty-seven now and lives in Baton Rouge. Lyn and Dee have three dogs and two pet pigs! She and her husband cherish their friends new and old and love to cook for anyone who comes by. Lyn enjoys being outdoors, lots and lots of reading, gardening in the early spring, and swimming.

ROBIN HEBERT grew up "a good little Catholic girl" in New Orleans, the youngest of three. The night her father died in a tragic airplane crash, her journey began. She was ten years old. She completed her Catholic education in New Orleans and attended the University of Southwestern Louisiana (now University of Louisiana–Lafayette), receiving both an undergraduate degree and a master's degree in Education.

Robin has been involved in ministry as a pastoral counselor, spiritual director, retreat leader, and professional speaker for more than twenty years. She has journeyed with hundreds who share her same desire for awareness and contemplative prayer. She now serves as a campus minister at Our Lady of Wisdom Catholic Church and Student Center on the University of Louisiana–Lafayette campus, offering her skills in spiritual direction, teaching prayer, and leading communities of students and parishioners in a deeper walk with God.

Past national president of Theresians of the U.S., a global ministry for women seeking a communal faith experience, Robin maintains involvement with Theresians through the mentorship of new communities and participation in her own "Open Heart" Community. Along with her husband, Easton, she co-leads annual mission trips for the Theresian World Ministry to a poor village in Mexico.

Robin and Easton live in Lafayette, Louisiana. They have been married for four years. She is a mother of four, stepmother of two, and grandmother of eight. Robin cherishes daily prayer time, walking, gardening, and reading. She is passionate about living a simple, balanced lifestyle.

Of Related Interest

Paula D'Arcy
A NEW SET OF EYES
Encountering the Hidden God

Through a series of meditations and parables, D'Arcy helps readers awaken the mind to the presence of God, free the soul from its cherished idols, and infuse the emotions with joy.

Today, like so many people, Paula D'Arcy is finding God apart from many of the traditional ways of experiencing spirituality. In the process, she catches glimpses of a God who is hidden and present at the same time, and shares those glimpses with her readers. *A New Set of Eyes* will be read and reread by those who are looking for a fresh perspective on their spiritual journey. It will also provide assurance and reminders that we are not alone on our collective quest. By the popular author of *Song for Sarah, The Gift of the Red Bird, Seeking with All My Heart,* and *Sacred Threshold.*

0-8245-1930-2, $16.95 hardcover

Please support your local bookstore,
or call 1-800-707-0670 for Customer Service.

For a free catalog, write us at

THE CROSSROAD PUBLISHING COMPANY
16 Penn Plaza, 481 Eighth Avenue
New York, NY 10001

Visit our website at
www.crossroadpublishing.com
All prices subject to change.

crossroad